THE WAR DIARIES OF U-764

FACT OR FICTION?

HEINZ F.K. GUSKE

THOMAS PUBLICATIONS
Gettysburg PA 17325

Printed and bound in the United States of America

Published by THOMAS PUBLICATIONS, Gettysburg, Pa. 17325

ISBN-0-939631-43-1

Front cover design by Ryan C. Stouch

Unless otherwise indicated, all photographs
are from the author's personal photo album.

Contents

List of Charts

Preface

Much has been written of and about U-boat warfare pertaining to the successes, failures, heroics, and the final surrender of those boats still remaining during World War II. Many details have been expounded by numerous authors from both sides of the former combatants, and there is no intention of adding to what has already appeared in print, as such. The objective here is to show quite a different side to it all, a side which very few people know of and which has not yet been published–at least not to my knowledge.

Some authors, war-correspondents in particular, may pretend, or even lay claim to being authorities on the subject. However, without any previous specialized training, no real work to do on board and just one guest-appearance under their belts, they know little or nothing of the realities. Though their stories may be entertaining to the layman, that does not equate with reliability or factuality.

Other accounts, mostly written by former U-boat commanders, carry much more convincing evidence; they are, indeed, accepted as totally authoritative, honest, and reliable. However, this view is not always totally justifiable. Frankly, I cannot be certain, for I have served under one U-boat commander only, and even the mere attempt of judging all others by the actions of this man would be utterly wrong. They may be of a singular nature, or they may not be, we shall probably never know. Nevertheless, we must take into consideration that the majority of books on the subject will be based upon the KTBs (War Diaries) of the boat, and the layman in particular will take it for granted that the entries therein will be unimpeachable.

Unimpeachable they may be, but that does not mean that they are correct. Evidence will be provided which illustrates that even the most informed members of U-boat Headquarters have been subjected to the falsifications of many KTBs. Consequently, it would be nearly impossible to spot any omissions in these documents without the consultation of a knowledgeable crew-member or the CO.

The CO of a U-boat can enter into and, even more so, omit from his KTB almost anything he may choose because he is the boss and there is no one to oppose him. There were only three people on U-764, who for certain, were privy to the contents of both the KTBs and the W/T-traffic in or out of the ship. These people were the CO, the 2WO and myself; the other officers may have had partial knowledge.

Whether the KTBs show the events at sea correctly or not (or some of those not at all) will not worry the CO in the least, for the other officers will, of course, keep their mouth shut for fear of jeopardizing their careers. I, myself, was in no position to expose any such falsifications or omissions then, for having to observe the procedure of "going through channels," the mere attempt would have been blocked immediately by either the 2WO or the CO. Besides, I would have been on my own, all documents would have been kept out of my reach, and it would then have been my word against his, whereas the CO would have received full support, right or wrong, from the other officers.

Though the crew would have had some knowledge of the events during the mission, they were otherwise restricted to whatever the CO deigned to impart, which may not be correct either. They had no access to the W/Ts or the KTB at all, and cannot know whether the entries in the latter are fact or fiction.

The staff at HQ would, of course, have had a copy of all W/T-traffic plus copies of the boat's KTBs submitted to them, but they had no knowledge of the actual occurrences during the mission. Even in the event of suspecting any irregularities in the KTB entries, they have no means of securing the proof thereof. The KTBs, therefore, would be accepted as they stood, and the CO remained untouchable.

That was the position then, but circumstances have changed a great deal in the meantime.

In the summer of 1985 (having had no contact with any crew member of U-764, nor having even had the slightest knowledge of activities pertaining to the former U-boat arm at all), I had, by chance, obtained a copy of the June 1984 issue of the German U-boat magazine titled *Schaltung Kueste*. To my utter amazement, I learned that the former CO had written a book about the missions of U-764 and its crew, based upon the copies of his KTBs, and that copies of the book had been distributed amongst those still surviving members of the crew, who were present at that year's reunion.

At that time, he did not know whether I was still alive, or if so, where I might be (nor for that matter, did any other member of the crew), and he obviously took it for granted to be safe from any contradiction or exposure. After all, as I have already pointed out, apart from the 2WO and possibly the other officers, the crew (with the exception of myself) had no access to the contents of the W/T-traffic or the KTBs.

It follows that he would have felt safe in the belief that he could put anything at all into his book (repeating the falsifications of his KTBs plus embroidering same as he saw fit) in the knowledge that at least the former 2WO would back him up should anyone dare question any statements made therein.

Indeed, Egbert Kandler, the 2WO, had already done so by publishing a paragraph in the June 1985 issue of *Schaltung Kueste* (No. 103), which is a very clever mix of fact, falsehood, and omission, in order to mislead the uninitiated and to provide support for any statement that the author of said book may have made. Since there is no KTB for the last mission in existence, he can make up any story he deems suitable for the occasion without fear of contradicting himself by any written statements made previously.

The translation of Kandler's paragraph reads:

> U-764, commissioned 6 May 1943, was on its 7th mission in the operational area North Minch, when the cessation of hostilities was made known by W/T on 8 May 1945. As we still had contact with the enemy, we moved out of the area in the direction of Norway, and on 13 May, when no further enemy action would be expected, we surfaced to the north of the Shetland Islands. A British search plane then ordered us to make for Loch Eriboll. The journey continued via Loch Alsh to Londonderry. U-764 has subsequently been sunk in accordance with operation *Deadlight*, and the crew, having been held captive for three years, returned home.

The underlined statements are false; in fact, just as false as the statements made by the CO to the British authorities upon surrendering the boat a week late. However, the quoted paragraph poses three questions: 1) What is the reason for publishing knowingly false statements some 40 years after the events; 2) Why publish same within a brief account of the reunion, which is usually confined to the names of the participants and any activities during the meeting, and are, therefore, totally out of place; 3) Why publish 12 months after distribution of the former CO's book, when the crew would be expected to be familiar with his stories anyway.

Although I do not know the answers, the most likely explanation would probably be that one of the former Petty Officers had already questioned the validity of certain statements made thereto in said book. This would have resulted out of the fact that Officers and NCOs had been called to the PO's room for a conference (behind closed doors with the remainder of the crew being excluded) on 8 May, when the CO announced his self-serving ideas as to what to do subsequent to the ending of the war.

It is, therefore, reasonable to assume that Kandler made the quoted statements in order to provide support to anything written by the former

CO. This appears to be a cover up which will be documented further in Chapter Nine.

Naturally, I was curious to read the material that the CO had produced. After all, as his book is based upon his KTBs, and as I know that many of his important entries are false, while some relevant ones have been omitted altogether, it is patently obvious that his narrative cannot be anything but equally false.

The book is not available commercially, and I did not approach the author for a copy, as I knew beforehand that he would refuse, for obvious reasons. Therefore, I wrote to Walter Ritter (ex-torpedo mechanic), the organizer of the mentioned reunions, and asked him to either obtain a copy for me, or have his copy xeroxed at my expense, or to send his copy to me (again at my expense), so that I could make a copy for myself, returning his thereafter. Ritter initially replied that he would let von Bremen know of my "surfacing signal" and added that my request with regard to said book "will be okay." In spite of two further letters, containing, inter alia, a repeat of my request, I have received no response.

I then obtained the address of and wrote to Werner Schulz (PO-Telegraphist during the boat's first two missions), putting the same request to him, but he did not even favour me with the courtesy of a reply.

In addition, it appears that Horst Bredow, the former 2WO of U-288 and now director of the U-boat Archives in Cuxhaven, Germany, had written to von Bremen himself, requesting a copy of his book for inclusion in the archives. Bremen, however, refused to be compliant. When we consider that Horst Bredow has founded said archives and continually strives by extremely hard work and largely at his own expense to both expand its contents and to be of service to all and everyone, then one must question why von Bremen refused to cooperate with a fellow ex-U-boat officer in his life's work. Considering the extent of effort that was sacrificed by von Bremen in publishing his book, one must also question his reasoning for the limitation of its distribution.

Alas, I leave the reader to draw his own conclusions after the pursuance of my account.

The Author

Acknowledgements

Although this book is based upon my own experiences and the war diaries of U-764, it could not have been written without the help of others. Any errors herein are, however, entirely my own.

It is, therefore, incumbent upon myself to express my appreciation and very special thanks to R.M. Coppock of the Naval Branch, Ministry of Defence, London, who has gone out of his way to afford me all available research facilities and has given his time and assistance most generously and in every way possible.

Further thanks are due to the staff of the Public Records Office in Kew, London, for all their help and assistance, as well as T.P. Mulligan of the Military Reference Branch, National Archives in Washington, D.C.

For providing copyright photographs, I am indebted to the Imperial War Museum, London, and to the National Archives of Canada. And last, but by no means least, to my good friend John Lindop in Holly Bank, Cheshire.

Introduction

The Boat

U-764 was a type VIIc boat, built at the Naval Dockyards in Wilhelshaven and launched in 1943. It had a surface displacement of about 770 tons (517 Washington tons), a length of 67 m, 6 m at the beam and a draught of some 5 m.

Equipped with 2 x 1,400 hp diesel engines and 2 x 375 electric motors, it could reach speeds of 17 knots and 7.5 knots respectively. Fuel capacity of 113 tons permitted a range of 6,500 miles at 12 knots, or 8,850 miles at 10 knots. The maximum diving depth was in the region of 250 metres.

Armament consisted of 4 bow torpedo tubes and one tube at the stern; there were also 2 x twin 20 mm and one 37 mm AA-guns (as of January 1944). It carried a crew of about 50, including 4 or 5 Officers, 3 Warrant Officers, and 12 or 13 Petty Officers.

U-764 had been commissioned in May 1943 and, after working-up and trials in the Baltic Sea, sailed for its first mission on 26 October. At the end of this mission, it joined the 9th U-Flotilla in Brest, where it was fitted with a schnorkel in April 1944. Before the fall of Brest during the invasion, the boat (being on its 5th mission, in the Channel), had been ordered to Norway to join the 11th Flotilla in Bergen.

The boat usually carried 10 or 11 torpedoes, none of which had been fired during the 2nd, 3rd, 6th or 7th missions. It suffered damage by depth-charges from escorts and/or U-boat hunters during missions 1, 4, & 5; those during 4 & 5 having been particularly serious. In addition, attacks by aircraft during the first three missions caused some damage, but only of minimal nature.

U-764 survived, accumulating some 240 days at sea. On 14 May 1945, while on its 7th and final mission, it had been surrendered to the British Navy in Loch Eriboll, transferred the next day to Loch Alsh, and eventually sunk in the Atlantic during operation *Deadlight.*

The Commanding Officer

The CO of U-764, from commission to surrender, was Oberleutnant zur See Hanskurt von Bremen, who was born on 11 August 1918 in Goslar, Lower Saxony. As far as could be ascertained, he became a midshipman in July 1939, an ensign in December of that year, and had been promoted to Leutnant zur See in April 1941. He served as Watch Officer with the 12th Minesweeper Flotilla and from December 1941 to January 1943 as 1WO on U-598. He then attended the commanding officer's course, gained promotion to Oberleutnant and took command of U-764 in May 1943.

After the usual trials and exercises in the Baltic Sea, he took the boat on its first mission from 26 October to 11 December 1943. During this mission, he sailed from Kiel where he patrolled off the Azores and Spain. He then joined the 9th U-boat Flotilla in Brest. Since I had not been on board during this mission, I cannot make any comment thereon. The boat, however, appears to have been attacked several times by both gun-fire from the air and by the armament of destroyers while on the surface and by their depth-charges when below.

The CO laid claim to, and was credited with, having shot down one aircraft on 27 November and sinking one destroyer the following day. The downed aircraft appears to have been a Wellington bomber (O-Orange HF153 of 179 Squadron RAF), but that claim is not absolutely certain.

As for sinking a destroyer, there is no record of such loss. He did fire two torpedoes on that occasion and in due course vessels of *Escort Group 2* (probably the sloops HMS *Starling, Magpie* and *Wildgoose*) took up the hunt. According to the KTB, first two then three destroyers dropped depth-charges for well over two hours but did not achieve any success.

The convoy involved was SL-140/MKS-31, which consisted of sixty-six ships, and during the night of 27-28 November, U-boats had been believed to be in close contact. About nine attacks were made, but all were driven off without loss. No further attacks had been reported after November 29, although FW-A/Cs were thought to have reported the convoy on the 30th. All ships arrived in the UK on 6 & 7 December.

I joined the boat for its second and all subsequent missions, and I was struck right away by the CO's arrogance, superciliousness and less than professional bearing. It appeared that he had little or no regard for his crew. It goes without saying that he demanded absolute obedience and prompt execution of his orders both at sea and ashore, whereas he, himself, ignored the orders and directives issued by his superiors at U-boat HQ whenever it served his own purpose.

The CO's unprofessional attitude and manners became abundantly clear from the very beginning of the 2nd mission, from 17 January to 15 March 1944. This was the boat's longest patrol, from Brest to the Mid- & North-Atlantic and back to Brest, during which he gave the eleven torpedoes on board a two-month outing and returned them back to base again.

Had there been no targets, no blame could be attached to him for lack of action. However, when the boat met a convoy almost head-on, at night, and dived to find itself undetected right in the midst of the convoy, with targets in practically every direction, yet it did not fire a single "fish," then one must take a closer look at this man's performance and the stories that he told in his KTB.

The 3rd mission, from 18 to 28 May 1944, was the shortest. The boat had been fitted with a schnorkel and this was to be a special hush-hush operation into the West Channel. We had been directed hither and thither, but nothing much happened—except for the fact that we were attacked three times on one occasion by aircraft. This resulted in one of the attacker's bullets penetrating the tubing of the round-dipol aerial on the bridge which caused water to leak into the sound room and the 40-watt transmitter beneath the cable-duct.

After having been on six-hour standby, the boat sailed for its 4th mission from 6 to 23 June. It was intended to attack the invading fleet in the Channel. On the ninth, the CO fired five torpedoes within an hour, without having any data of the targets, except hydrophone bearings in four directions. He missed completely, which was just as well because approximately five hours earlier he had been warned by W/T that four German destroyers would be traveling through that very area during that particular night.

This is but one more incident showing both his total disregard of the warning issued, as well as his incompetence. The Chief of Operations expressed the same views in his added assessment of the mission, which was attached to the KTB.

Further false entries in his KTB were used to cover up the next example of his incompetence when he fired two torpedoes at HMS *Blackwood* on the fifteenth. She had been hit by one "fish" and sank later the following day. During this attack, the top of the conning tower briefly broke surface (but this was not mentioned in the KTB) which literally signaled our position, if the enemy had noticed, and invited a counter-attack. This attack promptly followed, which caused heavy damage and forced the boat to return to base. Upon consideration of the circumstances of these events, the boat should never have made port, but rather, perished right then. Furthermore, there were additional scathing remarks by Rear-Admiral Godt.

Some six weeks later, repairs having been completed, U-764 sailed into the Channel again for its 5th mission, from 6 August to 19 September

1944, and not to see Brest again. The events that followed were, overall, very much a repetition of the previous mission: wild shooting, heavy damage by D/Cs forcing termination of the mission, and false entries in the KTB in order to conceal his incompetence.

This time, he fired six torpedoes and obtained one hit which sunk the 638 ton SS *Coral*. However, he falsely claimed 1,500 tons, as well as sinking a tank landing craft.

In spite of the damage sustained during the later attack by U-boat hunters, we survived again, and the boat reached the 11th U-Flotilla in Bergen. Extensive repairs plus delays caused by further indirect enemy actions kept the boat idle for a period of fourteen weeks. We then sailed for our 6th mission which took place from 26 December 1944 to 4 February 1945.

We had been on the way to the Channel once more, when, at the southwest corner of Ireland, the CO ordered the boat down "for a sounding" which resulted in the compression of the exhaust conduit. He then broke off the mission, reversed course, and commenced the return journey to Bergen. A week later, he missed the chance of an attack on a three-funnel liner (which was later identified as the SS *Ile De France*) because he did not act in time. It is no concern of mine as to whether the liner was stopped, sunk, or whatever; it is my concern that he made yet another false KTB entry which blamed one of my hydrophone operators for his own laziness and incompetence.

Following the completion of further lengthy repair work, we finally sailed for the 7th mission which lasted from 26 April to our surrender on 13 May 1945, in the area of the Pentland Firth. There is, of course, no KTB for this period in existence, but the false statements made to the British naval authorities upon surrendering the boat do supply further proof regarding his falsifications. However, his were not the only false statements. As mentioned in the Preface, Egbert Kandler, the former 2WO, published a paragraph in the *Schaltung Kueste* in June 1985 which made representations with regard to the closing days of the last mission, that were obviously false.

Consequently, von Bremen joined the Federal German Navy sometime during the 1950s, and when he finally retired, he had attained the rank of Fregattenkapitaen (Captain, junior).

The Author

Heinz Guske was born on 3 April 1921 in Breslau, Silesia and joined the crew of U-764 as Petty Officer Telegraphist some 23 years later.

When conscription had been reintroduced in Germany on 16 March

The author on board the tanker Adria *in Trondheim, Norway, October 1940.*

The Adria *refuelling the heavy cruiser* Admiral Hipper, *December 1940.*

Adria *refuelling the battleship* Scharnhorst *in the Greenland Sea, 31 January 1941.*

The Adria *with the battleships* Scharnhorst *and* Gneisenau *in the Greenland Sea, about 31 January 1941.*

The Adria *in the docks at Antwerp, Belgium, 6 April 1941.*

On the occasion of Vice Admiral Doenitz's birthday, 16 September 1941. Heinz Guske (at right) played the accordion.

"Present arms" during the birthday parade for Vice Admiral Doenitz (left) with C-in-C Italian submarines, Admiral Parona (saluting), and the commander of the guard company, Lt. Cmdr. Weber (right), 16 September 1941.

C-in-C U-boats, Vice Admiral Doenitz (right) and C-in-C Italian submarines, Admiral Parona (left), outside the former's villa in Kernevel, Lorient, 16 September 1941.

Commander-in-Chief U-boats, Vice Admiral Doenitz, during his birthday celebration in Kernevel, 16 September 1941

Admiral Parona (left) congratulating Vice Admiral Doenitz (right) on 16 September 1941. Between the two, Captain Godt, Chief of Operations.

An unidentified U-boat leaving Lorient for its next mission, 1941.

The author as leading-operator (Funk Obergefreiter) at U-boat H.Q. in Kernevel/Lorient directing traffic to and from Wilhelmshaven, Borkum and all U boats in and out of their bases up to about 10° - 12° west. The photograph is from a clip shot in March 1942 by the War-Correspondent's Unit, and was used about a year later by the cinema newsreel in connection with footage of the war at sea. Incidentally, the same clip has also been used in the television shows, "The World at War" and in "Victory at Sea."

1935, service in the Army became inevitable. As I was not keen on this branch of the forces, I took advantage of the rule permitting a choice by volunteering for service before call-up was due. In February 1938, therefore, I applied for service in the Navy and, having undergone a number of tests and medicals, was accepted.

At the commencement of war, papers arrived commanding me to report for basic training on 10 January 1940 in Stralsund. This was followed by telegraphy and equipment training at the communications school in Aurich. Upon completion, I was posted to the radio station of the Commandpost East in Swinemuende, to gain practical experience. At the same time, training was provided on portable equipment to be used during projected operation *Sealion*, the invasion of England.

When this plan was shelved, a number of personnel were freed of their post, and I found myself on the way to Trondheim, where I arrived on 11 September 1940 to serve on the fleet tanker *Adria*. Between 13 September 1940 and 11 February 1941, she made four trips into the Greenland Sea, refueling both the heavy cruiser *Hipper* and the battleships *Gneisenau* and *Scharnhorst*.

Adria then traveled south to the dockyards in Antwerp for a refit, toward the end of which, on 11 June 1941, all communications personnel were disembarked. During the next five weeks, I was moved via Wilhelshaven and Hamburg to Neustadt, where I obtained the posting to the Command Centre U-boat HQ in Kernevel, Lorient.

From 18 July 1941 to 30 September 1942, I worked there as a leading telegraphist both in the cipher room and conducting W/T-traffic between HQ, two shore stations, and all U-boats on the way to and from the Atlantic bases up to about 10° - 15° west. There was also a short spell of duty at the transmitter station. In March 1942, HQ transferred to Paris, and on 1 October, a number of personnel, including myself, were posted to the HQ W/T-station Villescresnes near Paris, where I served until posted to the Petty Officers' School in Muerwick, on 29 March 1943.

After graduation and promotion, I had hoped for resumption of service in either Villescresnes or Paris, but that request was turned down. I was, instead, invited to stay on at Petty Officers' School as an instructor, but, having rejected that offer, I was sent to the U-boat training division in Gotenhafen for a four-week course. From there, I was sent back to Neustadt for some peripheral training while I awaited the next posting which sent me to France again, to the personnel reserve of the 9th U-Flotilla in Brest. I remained there from 1 September 1943 to 11 January 1944, and worked in the Flotilla Communications Office.

On 12 January 1944, I was posted to U-764, and it was my intention to employ all my knowledge and experience, in particular that accumulated during some 18 months service at U-boat HQ, to the best advantage of the boat's missions.

Chapter One

To the Operational Area

Second Mission
17 January to 15 March 1944

When U-764 arrived in Brest, the communications department (See Appendix 1) was manned by 1 PO-Telegraphist and 2 telegraph/ hydrophone operators, whereas there should have been a complement of 2 POs and 3 operators. In order to bring the department up to strength, Karl-Heinz Zarges and myself were posted from the flotilla's personnel reserve to this boat.

On 12 January, we went on board to report our posting to the CO who, at that time, was leaning against the railing of the upper wintergarden, flanked by the 2WO and the LI. We saluted and stood at attention until "looked at or spoken to," as per service regulations. The CO, however, chose to ignore us and did not deign returning our salute either then or subsequently. When he did finally acknowledge our presence by shifting his gaze in our direction, we made our report, and he asked where I had served previously. When I mentioned U-boat IIQ, he interjected that he had served there also, and that was it. There was no handshake or any other gesture of welcome, and the arrogance displayed by this man conveyed the message that, as far as I was concerned, I was on the wrong boat. Instinct told me that my intentions of putting the knowledge garnered and the experience gained to the best use and advantage of the boat's missions would be frustrated by this man, and my hunch was soon borne out as correct.

We sailed on 17 January at 1600, escorted by three minesweepers. The Second Flotilla Engineer was on board because we still had to carry out a deep diving test near the 200-metre-line, which had been reached by 0800 the following morning. The boat went slowly down to 180 metres and one or two minor problems were corrected during this time. When we surfaced again, at 1102, visibility had deteriorated badly and the escort boats were nowhere to be seen.

As per KTB entries 18-1-44

The escort had been sighted at 1300 but no radar bearings had been obtained in spite of the visibility being very bad, a mere 1-2 sm. Having completed the deep diving test, the Flotilla Engineer was transferred by dingy to the minesweeper, as he had to be taken back to Brest.

Facts

This entry is quite non-sensical, for the visibility (good, bad, or indifferent) has no influence upon obtaining a bearing by radar.

Comment/explanation

As the escort had been sighted, there was no earthly reason for using radar in the first place. Alternatively, it might be argued that this entry was meant to convey that in spite of the bad visibility, radar had not been used at all. If that was the case, then he should have expressed himself clearly. In fact, I have no recollection of our radar being used at all, but I do remember the Flotilla Engineer receiving a slight ducking during his transfer, as I happened to be on the upper wintergarden in readiness for assembling and lowering the first of 15 Thetis into the sea.

While traversing the Biscay, every night for the next six, one of the operators and myself assembled 2-3 Thetis on the quarter-deck and planted same at certain positions. The boat was on the surface for 2 and 1/2 to 3 hours each night, recharging the batteries in what were reputed to be very dangerous waters, closely monitored by A/S-patrols of RAF Coastal Command. Yet, we neither detected any radar search by air or sea nor was there any surprise attack by plane or surface vessel. All was quiet and appeared very unreal and eerie.

As per KTB entries 27-1-44

The communications frequency had been changed to the Diana service at 0400, but our W/T 0805, transmitted at 0824, had been entered with the serial number 9.

Facts

We had been on the Diana service for more than 4 hours by the time this W/T went out. This means that the W/T transmitted should have had a serial number between 701 and 800. The number 9 identifies the Coastal service (whose numbers run from 1 to 100) and was, therefore, falsely entered.

Comment/explanation

Incompetent log-keeping.

As per KTB entries 29-1-44

At 1817, the W/T 1712/29/734 had been received. Seventy minutes later, however, at 1927, the CO stated that the W/Ts, bearing the serial numbers 725 & 729, had been cancelled by W/T 1712/29/234.

Facts

The number 734 is surely plain enough and the correct one for the Diana service. The number 234 for the very same W/T is, therefore, again falsely entered.

Comment/explanation

More incompetent log-keeping.

The reader may now take the view that the inclusion of these two entries is unwarranted on the grounds of triviality. If those were the only such entries, I would agree completely; they are not. There are many, many more of a similar nature and, taken together, they will provide evidence of falsity throughout, extremely sloppy log-keeping, and plain incompetence.

As per KTB entries 31-1-44

Our Naxos aerial detected radar search on two occasions, at 0700 and at 0740. Less than 48 hours later, on 2 February, we are told that due to a broken ceramic-rod, the Naxos aerial has ceased to function at 0400. The blame for this is then extended by accusing the fitting-out department of having delivered *both* aerials with their rods broken.

Facts

The final statement of 2 February is false because 1) each boat is supplied with one aerial only, plus one spare ceramic-rod; 2) the rod fitted worked quite satisfactorily, as is shown by the entry of the 31st, when radar search had been detected on two occasions, thus proving that the fitted one at least had not been supplied defective in any way; 3) breaking of the rod fitted did not occur out of the blue at 0400, as it is made to appear, but was due to the aerial being dropped from the bridge right down into the control room when diving; 4) when the replacement rod had been unwrapped, it was found that same was indeed broken, but there was no evidence to show when or how this may have happened; 5) although the CO had noted the damage to the aerial in the KTB, albeit in a manner not consistent with the facts, he should have also entered the fact that repairs had been made, rendering the aerial operative again by different means.

Comment/explanation

This is yet another example of the unprofessional behavior of the CO. He passed the blame of the problem on to the supply department rather than handling the situation himself. In addition, the entry is inconsistent with proper log-keeping because it is incomplete. He did not subsequently enter the successful repair of the aerial, as this would have defeated his objective of showing the communications department in a bad light.

Incidentally, a number of other boats had also reported breakage of the ceramic-rods, and recorded their own manners of repairs, and whether or not they were successful. The repair of our aerial should have also been entered for the benefit of other boats.

As per KTB entries 2-2-44

The etmal at 1200 is given as 116.5 sm for surface travel, 138.4 sm for submerged travel, and the total is stated as 138.4 sm.

Facts

The figure for submerged travel is quite ludicrous because, having been below for 11 and 1/4 hours, same is equivalent to a speed of 12.3 knots, which is impossible because it exceeds the attainable top speed by 64%. Apart from that, the average distance traveled submerged is roughly 26 sm per day during the last fifteen days.

Comment/explanation

Another example of incompetent log-keeping.

The CO also displays his incompetence in the figure of 138.4 sm for its total; the sum of the figures stated comes to an undisputable 254.9 sm. Furthermore, the emergency repairs to the Naxos aerial not only worked well, as the following KTB entries will show, but the idea, which is mentioned in my reports for the benefit of any other PO in a similar situation, had been taken up and later issues of this aerial had been fitted with a solid rod of copper, instead of the original, rather fragile, ceramic one.

Chapter Two

Surprised by Convoy ON-222

As per KTB entries 3-2-44

At 2000, the boat was on the surface in AL 9982 and traveling north on a course of 345° true, in order to reach the previously stipulated patrol position in AL 9293 by using the most economical speed.

The weather was fine with a light breeze from the west, force 1-2, a long medium swell from the same direction plus good visibility.

An hour later, at 2100, radar pulses were being picked up by our Naxos aerial and, in spite of launching Aphrodite three times, the radar search continued. In fact, the pulses gained in both clarity and volume, occurring at intervals of three to five seconds. Half an hour thereafter, the boat submerged and a subsequent search by hydrophone revealed propeller noises in 55° and 340° true, which turned out to be those of destroyers. Those noises then moved off, and it was assumed that the destroyers were now reacting to the bearings obtained on the previously launched Aphrodites. Further propeller noises were being picked up at 2200, on a bearing of 40° true and, between 2234 and 2310, the submerged boat was being overrun by a convoy on a southerly course.

Facts

Both this and the following part of the entries are disputable.

At the first detection of radar search at 2100, the distance between boat and destroyers would have been in the region of 8 sm, the inclination was almost head-to-head, and the closing speed was approximately 14 knots. This meant that the destroyers were practically on top of us and should have detected, if not actually seen, the boat by the time it submerged half an hour later, at 2133. Yet it took another hour before the convoy overran the submerged boat at 2234, and the passage itself required thirty-six minutes.

Whatever the mathematics of this incomprehensible nonsense, the facts remain: the boat found itself at night, undetected, within the convoy, and targets were presented in nearly every direction; clearly a situation that most COs can only dream of. However, our boat merely hung there, some fifty metres below the surface, while the convoy could be heard, unaided, passing overhead. But the CO made no move!

It should be noted that the escorts did not use their Asdic for underwater location, nor had they streamed their CATs.

Comment/explanation

The destroyers were obviously on permanent radar search, which means that our Naxos installation had picked up their pulses as soon as they cleared the horizon. They thus revealed their presence without detecting the target because of the boat's bow on inclination, showing the smallest silhouette. At that stage, the top of the conning tower would be level with the horizon, at a distance of about 8 sm from the destroyers' radar, and detection would have been most unlikely. Indeed, there is no evidence of the boat having been detected at all.

The CO continued on his head-to-head course and was, simultaneously, advertising our presence by the launching of Aphrodites three times before getting out of the convoy's path by going below some thirty minutes later. He then reemerged again once the convoy had passed overhead.

If these are the actions of a "competent" and "attack-spirited" CO (as he had been described), then I would be very much interested to know what an *incompetent* one would have done under these circumstances!

As per KTB entries 4-2-44

The soundband of the convoy, while still audible, had decreased considerably, and the boat surfaced in AL 9985 at 0006. The weather situation had not changed during the past four hours, except that the good visibility had now been augmented by the light of the moon.

At 0009, the CO ordered transmission of a convoy report by W/T 2342 of 3 February. Therein he stated having observed continuing radar search since 2100 and that the boat had been overrun by a south-bound convoy in AL 9955 at 2300. We are then told that a large shadow and the rear escort, consisting of two destroyers, could be seen ahead of the boat. He then stated his intention as traveling up the convoy's moon-lee flank in order to gain a forward position and penetrating the convoy from the front. An hour later, by means of the B-Bar signal at 0108, he reported the convoy to be in AL 9975 and proceeding on a course of 220° true. A cloud or the reflected light of the moon now and again obscured sight of the convoy, whereas the rear escort and the straggler were said to have drifted astern at 0130. We are then told that one destroyer was covering the convoy's port side, and beyond her, four largish shadows could be seen.

As per the CO's estimate, the convoy consisted of five steamers and a protecting escort of six destroyers. Two of those, searching the surface with their radar, were leading the van, two more were at the convoy's flank (meaning, presumably, one on either side) and the remaining two were covering the rear.

While the boat was alleged to be athwart the convoy, the Naxos aerial picked up radar search again at 0147. The escort on the convoy's port side was then said to be at a distance of 6,000 metres and turning her bow in the direction of the boat.

The convoy, in the meantime, again disappeared intermittently from view in a dark cloud to the west, whereas the boat had a clear sky to the east behind it and was silhouetted against the horizon. He, therefore, ran off at full speed, but the destroyer did not react to the Aphrodite and the distance between her and the boat remained the same. It is also said that the destroyer presented her beam every quarter hour, but then turned bow-on, toward the boat again. Brightness prevented the CO from closing in on her. He briefly reported this point by the next B-bar signal at 0208, saying that he was being forced away by a destroyer.

At 0245, the visibility had diminished slightly, and the destroyer had disappeared. While the CO was operating upon the convoy's course, he stated that no bearing was obtainable on the D/F-frequency. The searchlight of an aircraft was seen close to the boat at 0307, barely 500 metres from our stern, but there was no attack. Further radar pulses were picked up a few minutes later and Aphrodite was sent aloft again.

At 0315, the W/T 0250 was received, addressed to *Group Igel*. The CO was thereby ordered to transmit continuous contact reports and was given a free hand to attack this convoy. Other boats of the group were urged to join in at maximum speed, provided they were in such a position as to reach the convoy in the course of the day. These orders were closely followed by W/T 0253, which amplified the previous one by assuming the convoy to be America-bound and to be traveling at some 8-9 knots on a southwesterly course.

At both 0351 and 0400, in BE 2314 and with medium visibility, further radar pulses were being picked up and it was assumed that they were being emitted by an aircraft as there was nothing else in sight. The boat, according to dead-reckoning, had now reached the front of the convoy and was taken below to carry out a hydrophone search. This revealed an extensive noiseband astern of the boat and a destroyer in 295° true. The main-bearing was then said to be shifting slowly to port, thus putting the boat on the starboard side of the convoy. At this point, however, the CO intended to penetrate the convoy from the rear, since there had been less aggression by the destroyers at the stern while he was dashing to the front.

Some ninety minutes thereafter, at 0528, the convoy had moved out to 110° true, while one of the destroyers was still audible at volume 1-2 in 275° true. The boat then surfaced in bad visibility, and as the radar search was still continuing, a further Aphrodite had been launched. At 0532, he ordered transmission of W/T 0500, stating that hydrophone bearings placed the convoy in BE 2315 and radar pulses were continuously being detected whenever the boat was closing the convoy.

Immediately upon acknowledgement of this W/T having been received, the boat was ordered below again to avoid being surprised by a destroyer during the bad visibility. He then intended to wait until the destroyer had moved out of audible range so that he could follow up. However, two hours later, the destroyer was still being heard making a search of the area.

He stayed below in BE 2314, and at 0800 broke off any further operation during the day because the 37 mm AA-gun was out of action. By this time, the destroyer had moved off and was no longer audible. The boat then turned north again toward the previously ordered patrol position, steering a course of 358° true. W/T 0816 then followed, which ordered all boats near this convoy to remain on the surface, to keep an eye on the situation and to attack, instead of allowing themselves to be forced under by mere radar search without having sight of the enemy.

Facts

Having idly let the convoy pass overhead, the boat was, at this point, on the surface, traveling along behind the two destroyers covering the rear. At about 0030, the call came through: "Radio room! PO-Telegraphist report to the bridge!" Responding as ordered, the CO asked me whether the three short signals were ready for transmission. Receiving an affirmative reply, he said nothing further.

Incidentally, standing orders decreed three short signals to be ready for instant transmission before the boat had surfaced:

"Being attacked by Destroyer" + position & signature
"Being attacked by Aircraft" + position & signature

"Convoy in position..." + signature.

While on the bridge, I took the rare opportunity of having a look at the situation; I could hardly believe what I saw. We were not so much *behind* the two rear escorts, but practically *amongst* them! The sea was calm, the sky was overcast to about 6/10. The boat was in the dark under cover of the clouds. On our port side, in about 280° from us, also in the dark, was the shadow of a destroyer to be seen at a distance of some 3,000 metres. On our starboard side, in about 80° from us, fully illuminated by the moon, was the second destroyer at a distance also of about 3,000 metres.

Returning to the radio room, I assumed the CO would be mounting an attack upon these destroyers and possibly expecting a counter-attack. Hence, his question regarding the short signals. There was, however, no attack upon either the escorts or the convoy at any time. Indeed, he could not have even fired a torpedo in self-defence, for none of the tubes had been flooded and the bow-caps remained closed.

In spite of the later signal "being forced away by destroyer," nothing appeared to be happening. Being in the radio room, I had, of course, no direct knowledge of the subsequent developments outside, but I was not aware of any evasive actions or other counter-measures being taken; we just seemed to be traveling along as before.

The next false entry was made at 0245 when he claimed to be operating upon the convoy's course but that no bearing was obtainable on the D/F-frequency. That statement is certainly false. The direction finder, as far as I recall, had not been used, since there was no need for so doing in the first place. He knew where the convoy was and he was "operating upon its course" (at least according to his KTB). His *operation* was ludicrous and unbelievable in any event. This is just another story that he fabricated in order to conceal his incompetence. Consequently, he did, in fact, succeed in deceiving HQ.

Pure luck had already placed us in the most advantageous position imaginable by first being right in front of the convoy, then inside and below same, at night and undetected, with targets in every direction; yet, the CO took no action whatsoever. We must also take into consideration that at that time, it was taken as quite an achievement if a U-boat managed to penetrate a convoy's defences at all. Furthermore, if a convoy was found (which was a rare occurrence in 1944), the CO was to attack at once and make a report about it afterwards. This CO, however, neither took advantage of the situation, nor carried out the orders given.

Having been in front of the convoy and then finding himself on the surface between the rear escorts, he stated his intention, at 0009, as "reaching for a forward position and penetrating the convoy from the front." Some four hours later, at 0407, having allegedly reached a forward sector, he came up with another idea: he intended to get into the convoy from the rear, and thus asserting his incompetence once again. Furthermore, this intention was soon cast aside as well. After all his dashing forwards and backwards again (at least per his KTB entries), he appeared to have lost sight of what he was doing, and whether he was coming or going. Some ninety minutes later, at 0535, he put forward yet a third intention, which was to wait until the destroyer was out of audible range, and then follow up. At this point, he had nothing left to follow up.

Comment/explanation

By the time this man sorted himself out and made up his mind as to what course of action to adopt, there would not be anything left for him to follow up. The convoy would have moved further ahead and the escorts would have prevented him from gaining contact again during daylight. In addition, they would attack the boat with every available weapon. At dawn, one and one-half hours later, he finally broke off his operation on the mere grounds of "an inoperative 37 mm anti-aircraft gun"!

The story, as told in the KTB and thus the one he wanted HQ to believe was based upon the following facts:

3 February

2100 Detected radar search and advertised the boat's presence by launching Aphrodite three times

2133 Dived and obtained hydrophone bearings in 55° and 340° true

2200 Further hydrophone bearings in 40° true

2234 to 2310 Overran by convoy on southerly course

4 February

0006 Surfaced astern of convoy amongst two rear escorts

0009 Reported convoy and its position by short W/T

0108 Further report of convoy by B-bar signal

0208 B-bar stating "Forced away by destroyer"

0532 Short W/T giving convoy's position as per hydrophone bearings

0800 Broke off operation

These facts were then coupled with the composition of the convoy as had been presumed by the CO. The convoy consisted of 2 destroyers leading,the van, followed by 5 merchantmen with a flank escort of 2 more destroyers plus 2 further destroyers covering the rear. This convoy then overran the boat in thirty-six minutes, and at a speed of 8-9 knots, the convoy would have been 4-5 miles in length. When we surfaced an hour later, at 0006, the convoy would have been on or beyond the southern horizon. However, when I was called to the bridge about thirty minutes after surfacing, the boat was practically abreast of the two stern sweepers.

The staff at HQ should have noticed that a) even the Allies' material superiority would have hardly allowed for five merchantmen to be escorted by six destroyers, and certainly not in the Atlantic. The run to Malta in the Mediterranean was, of course, governed by quite different circumstances, calling for much stronger protective measures; b) a convoy of five merchantmen would not be sailing in single file, but would adopt a three-abreast followed by a two-abreast configuration. This permitted the six escorts to form a much tighter protective ring and the time of passage past or over a U-boat lurking submerged would be halved as well, thereby decreasing the possibility of a successful attack still further; and c) the widely separated hydrophone bearing on the propeller noises of the destroyers leading the van (i.e. 55°, 340° plus 40°) surely point to something much more substantial than had been *presumed* by this CO. However, before dealing with the realities of the situation, there are his entries as to position and bearings to be considered.

In order to give the reader a better overall view, Chart 1 shows the route traveled by U-764 between 28 January and 26 February 1944, as per KTB entries. Also shown is the median course of convoy ON-222. The enlarged Chart 2 illustrates the events of 2-4 February, as per the story told in the KTB. In order to avoid confusion, all positions are given as per the German Naval Grid Square System (see Appendix 2). These notations will be added to the latitude x longitude of the convoys, as per the British records.

On 2 February, for example, the CO gave his position as AL 9995 and steering a course of 80° true. Two and one-half hours later, however, at 2235, he was on a heading of 300° true. Yet, some ninety minutes later, at 0000 of the third, he stated his position to be in AM 7772. In other words, he was steering a northwesterly course, yet shifted his position in an easterly direction.

Equally false are the following entries: At 1600, on 3 February, he was in AL 9982; four hours later, at 2000, he was still there. Having surfaced, we were then traveling on a course of 345° true until diving at 2133. During those ninety minutes, the boat would have advanced by roughly 10 miles in a northerly direction, placing it into AL 9955, where same had been overrun by the convoy. During the two and one-half hours that elapsed from diving to surfacing again, at 0006 on 4 February, the boat would have moved very little (5 miles, perhaps), but it was more than 15 miles to the south, in AL 9985. Yet, the W/T at 0009 reported that he had been overrun by a south-bound convoy, at 2300, in AL 9955. It would have been impossible for him to have traveled some 15 miles submerged in an hour, when the attainable top speed is only half of that. The convoy, in the meantime, had moved on, and to be in AL 9975 by 0100 (as per the B-bar 0108), would have to have been just crossing from AL 9957 into AL 9973, at 0000. If this were correct, then the boat would be some 10 miles to the south-southeast of the convoy's port side. Yet, when I was called to the bridge, we were amongst the two rear escorts.

In addition, if the convoy were to traverse the distance from AL 9955 to AL 9975 in two hours, a speed of 11-12 knots would have been required, which is out of the question. However, let us assume that he was in AL 9985 at 0000 on the fourth. In order to reach the position of BE 2314, as stated for 0400, he would have had to have been traveling parallel to the convoy, at about 10 miles distance on its port side, and covering some 30 miles. Thirty miles in four hours equates a speed of 7.5 knots, and as the convoy was proceeding at 8 knots, he could not possibly "reach a forward sector" as he stated in his Intention at 0009.

Obviously, matters are becoming more complicated and the evidence of his falsifications is becoming more apparent.

At 0407, the boat, according to dead-reckoning, was in front of the convoy and submerged for a hydrophone search. The bearings thus obtained on the sound-source were said to be shifting slowly to port and the boat was therefore on the convoy's starboard side. Therefore, traveling at about 7.5 knots, he had overtaken the convoy, which was moving ahead at some 8 knots. Not only that, he had also bridged the 10-15 miles distance between the boat and the convoy by moving right across its path from the port side to the starboard flank—or so we are lead to believe. Obviously, this could not have been achieved. Nevertheless, this CO solves the problem very neatly with W/T 0500; he simply placed the convoy into BE 2315. In other words, he *made* the convoy execute a change of course from 220° to 180° and reduced its speed from 8 knots to 4.5. By this simple expedient, the boat is now on the convoy's starboard side and the latter is in 110° true, at a distance of about 4-5 miles. This also covers for his stated intention of getting into the convoy from the rear.

His account, according to the KTB, is obviously false. Furthermore, in order to produce a convincing end to his situation, he first stated, at 0535, his intention of "waiting until the destroyer is out of audible range and then follow[ing] up," and having been *waiting* for ninety minutes (during which the convoy would have disappeared over the horizon), he broke off operating by day, since the 37 mm AA-gun was out of order.

Route travelled by U-764 between 27 January and 25 February 1944, as per the KTB. It does not take into account any discrepancies vis-a-vis the course steered.

Position at (German time):

0800 = —— ■ ——

2000 = —— ❍ ——

between = —— • ——

Convoy positions at (GMT):

0800 = — — ⬭ — —

Chart One

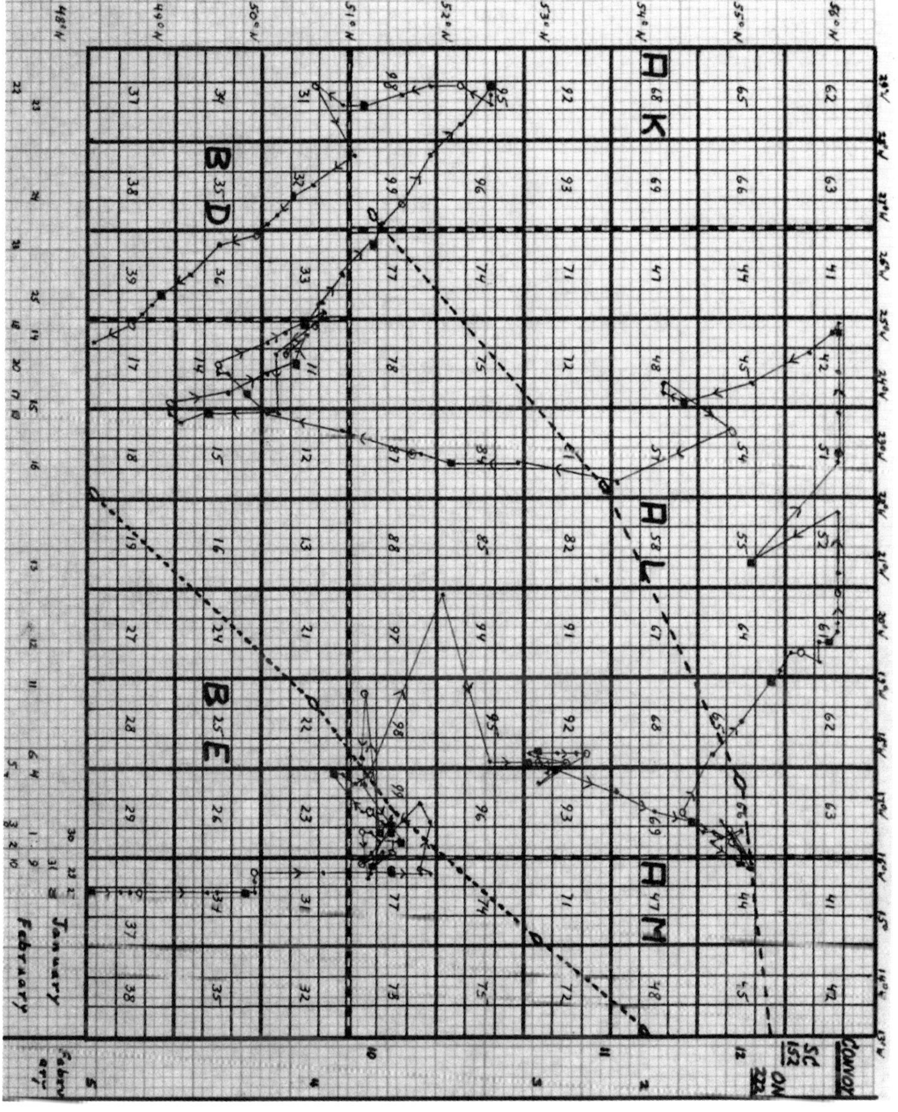

Chart Two shows the positions of both U-764 and Convoy ON-222, as per the KTB entries.

Chart Three shows the true positions of both boat and convoy, as per the British records.

These positions are further underlined by the W/T of U-963 (Boddenberg), which reported to have attacked this convoy in BE 2225, at 0750, on 4 February. His own position was correctly D/F'd by HMS *Ottawa* (see text).

Chart Two

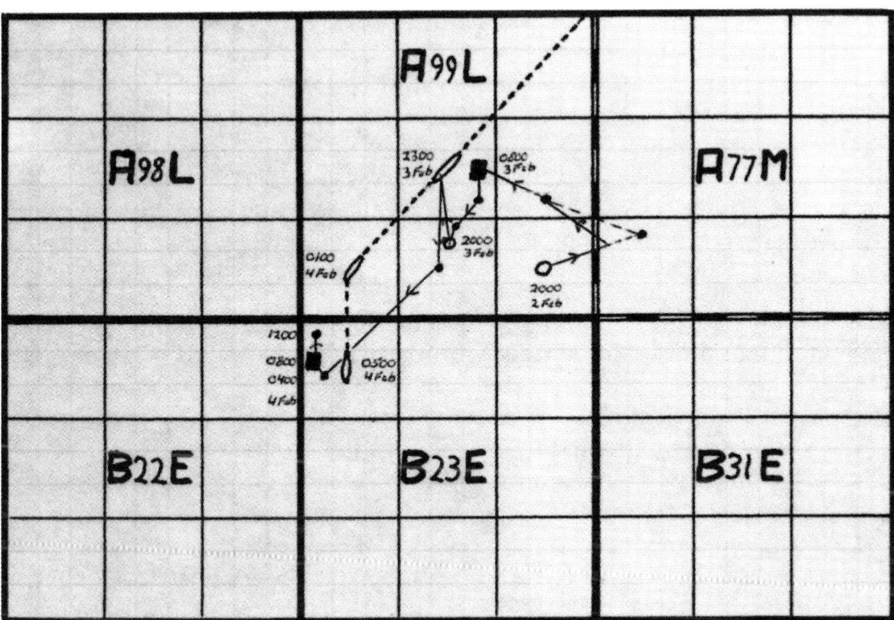

Chart Three

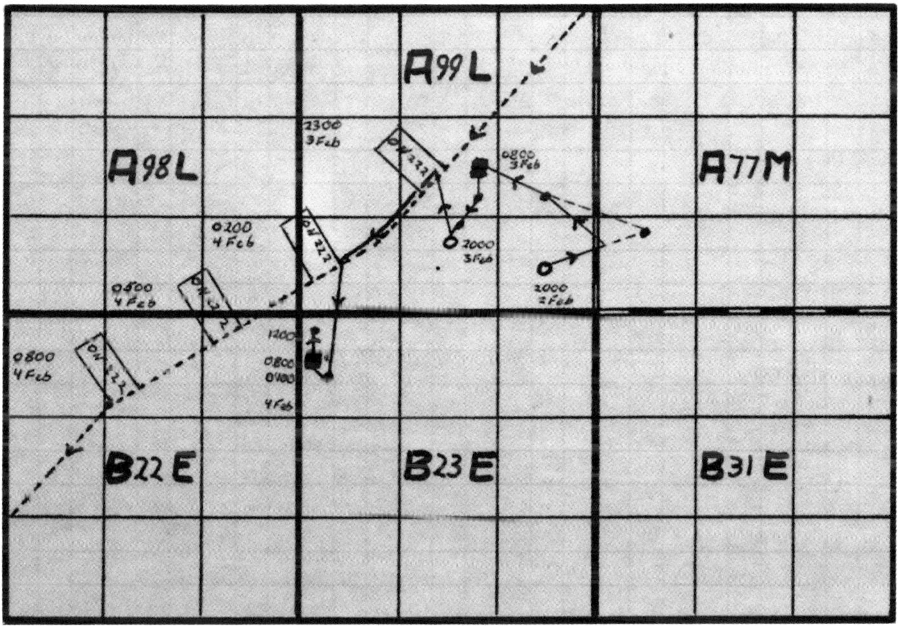

If the personnel at HQ had plotted the KTB's data onto some larger scale squared paper (as Chart 2, for example), they should have become aware that the story told was pure fabrication. Evidently, they produced no such plot and in consequence had been utterly deceived. This is clearly reflected in the opinion given by Rear-Admiral Godt, the Chief of Operations, when he said that

> the boat, having reached the front of the convoy after much effort, had been deprived of success on account of the bad visibility at the decisive moment. But there had been opportunity to shoot without sight, by using hydrophone bearings, from a depth of sixty metres when the boat was being overrun by the convoy. Although this attack-spirited CO attempted to obtain a firing position, success, alas, could not be achieved.

When Rear-Admiral Godt used the term "attack-spirited," it showed the extent to which both he and the staff at HQ had been deceived. Clearly, there was no such "spirit" in evidence during the events in question. The CO could , for example, have fired two FATs (one with a left loop and one looping to the right) while undetected and below the convoy, keeping one T5 (GNAT) for each of the stern sweepers and one remaining T5 for defence against a counter-attack by any of the other escorts.

Furthermore, after surfacing between the two rear escorts, he may have been able to fire one T5 at each of them; he had all the necessary data: speed of and distance and angle to both targets. And, since they had not streamed their CATs, the T5s should have found their mark. He could then, possibly, have sent two FATs chasing the convoy and, even if he did not score there, two end-of-run detonations together with the hits on the two rear escorts should have caused sufficient confusion for an escape at top speed on the surface before diving out of sight at a considerable distance. But, as indicated already, no such "attacking spirit" was in evidence.

The story, thus far, however, is based on the composition of the convoy as presumed by the CO: 5 Merchantmen traveling in single file, being protected by six escorts. The question remains as to the reliability of this data, and whether his presumption is correct or not.

There is no doubt that we had been overrun by a column of ships plus two, possibly three, escorts, but each of those five merchantmen had nine neighbors in line abreast on its starboard side. This was, in fact, a convoy of forty-nine ships plus two stragglers (one of which caught up on the morning of the fourth), protected by seven escorts and one MAC plus a support group of three U-boat hunters. If the disposition of the escorts had been as the CO had presumed (six of them guarding five merchantmen), then the main-body of the convoy would have been

HMCS Ottawa *(courtesy of Canadian Forces)*

HMCS Dunver *(courtesy of Canadian Forces)*

totally unprotected and left wide open to attack, particularly on the starboard side. This is, of course, utterly absurd.

Facts

We had been overrun by the port wing of Convoy ON-222, sailing with 50-51 merchantmen from the UK on 30 January and arriving at its destination on 16 February without loss.

The position of this convoy for the period in question was, at 0800 GMT, as follows:

3 Feb.	AM 7196	(52:57N x 14:35W),	7 knots
4 Feb.	BE 2243	(50:38N x 18:38W),	9 knots
5 Feb.	BE 1899	(48:20N x 22:05W),	9 knots

Ocean Escort	2 Destroyers	:	*Ottawa, Kootenay*
	1 Frigate	:	*Dunver*
	4 Corvettes	:	*Rosthern, Dianthus, Dauphin, Summerside*
	1 MAC	:	*Empire Macrae*
Support Group C2	2 Frigates	:	*Keats, St. Catherines*
	1 Corvette	:	*Fennel*

The Ocean Escort was stationed around the convoy at distance of 5,000 yards from it, and the MAC, carrying four swordfish, being placed abeam of the rear ships in adjacent columns. At the time U-764 encountered this convoy, the Canadian Support Group was leading the van about a mile ahead of the Ocean Escort, with HMCS *Keats* occupying the centre position and HMCS *Fennel* and HMCS *St. Catherines* at three and six miles respectively on her starboard beam.

In spite of their radar search and the launched Aphrodite, our presence had neither been detected nor even suspected. Thus, we went below, were overrun by the convoy, resurfaced between HMCS *Ottawa* and HMCS *Dunver* at 0006 on 4 February and they still were quite oblivious of our presence. This can only be described as luck!! However, British records (ADM 199/70) give their own account of the events, and they reveal what had not been known before.

For example, on 4 February, at 0009, HMCS *Ottawa* immediately picked up our W/T (reporting the convoy) on a bearing of 85° from her, but unaccountably placed the transmission at over 30 miles away. It was, therefore, assumed that this W/T reported one of the stragglers and no action had been taken. An hour later, at 0108, HMCS *Ottawa* D/F'd our next transmission in 135° from her and the B-bar was thought, quite correctly, to be a sighting report of this convoy. But, no counter-measures followed, as a decision had been taken to wait for one hour, in order to see whether or not any further amplifying report may be made. Exactly one hour later, at 0208, HMCS *Ottawa* again picked up our next B-bar at a bearing of 125° from her, and at the same time, HMCS *Dunver* obtained a radar contact in 100° true at a distance of 3.5 miles. Seven minutes later, however, the radar contact was reported to have been a false alarm.

Nevertheless, suspicions at least had been aroused and at 0222, the order went out to HMCS *Dunver* to undertake a search on a course of 125° true to a distance of 15 miles. This was followed by ordering the Senior Officer of the 2nd Canadian Escort Group to sweep down the port side of the convoy and to search for the U-boat, particularly at sections B & C. The convoy was at that time traveling at 9 knots on a course of 235° true.

By this time, it had also been realized that the bearings obtained by H/F D/F were not as good as they might have been, but an estimate, at 0435, did place a U-boat in 91° true, ZZ31. *Empire Macrae* had been informed of the situation at that time with the order to fly off two of her aircraft at daybreak. One had the task of locating and dealing with the U-boat on their tail, the other was to fly around the convoy in a Viper-patrol.

Another hour had passed when, at 0531, HMCS *Ottawa's* H/F D/F again picked up a Naval Enigma W/T on a bearing of 91° from her. The Senior Officer of the Canadian Support Group, who had been sweeping the port side of the convoy, was then ordered to extend his search to a distance of 25 miles on a course of 53° true. This search also produced no result and at 0824, the group was ordered to return to the convoy. In the meantime, at 0811, HMCS *Ottawa* had D/F'd yet another B-bar in 330° from her. On this occasion it was HMCS *Dunver's* turn to go hunting along this bearing to a distance of 15 miles. She was recalled at 0900, but before rejoining, she was to search astern of the convoy to a depth of 5 miles.

As on all other occasions, there was no sign of a U boat. Yet, at 0907, a U-boat was again heard transmitting at 16° from HMCS *Ottawa*, more than 30 miles away. By this time, the previously ordered aircraft from the MAC were aloft (A/S search had been carried out from 0750 to 1115, the Viper-patrol from 0820 to 0950), therefore, no further action was deemed necessary.

These facts supply clear proof of U-764's KTB having been fabricated. Although the entries of both W/Ts and the B-bars are correct (they had to be, otherwise HQ, who had copies of them, would surely have suspected a problem), everything else is false.

Comment/explanation

There is no doubt that HQ had been totally fooled by this CO's story as told in his KTB, and it would not surprise me in the least if the reader would also be led to believe what he entered. To see the events clearly, it is, therefore, necessary to put the KTB entries in line with the actual facts. The reader must bear with me as many repetitions will occur during this process.

To begin with, on 3 February at 2000, the boat was in AL 9982, steering a course of 345° true. At 2133 it went below and was overrun by the convoy between 2234 and 2310 in AL 9955. Some fifty minutes later, however, at 0000 of the fourth, the boat was still below, but was now said to be in AL 9985. It is impossible to comprehend how he could have computed 12-14 miles traveled, while submerged, in one hour.

Prior to this, at 2100, continuous radar pulses had been detected which, by the very nature, could only have been emitted by surface vessels. These vessels would, at that stage, be at a distance of about 8 miles and the boat, by its bow-on inclination, would be almost impossible to detect. One may only speculate as to why he chose to advertise our presence by launching Aphrodite three times.

The boat was then overrun by this convoy, was some fifty metres below same without having been detected by either radar while on the surface and in front, or by asdic (which, in fact, had not been used) while submerged. This was a perfect setting for a surprise attack, but there was no action by this CO.

At 0006 on 4 February, we surfaced between the two sterns sweepers, yet our presence there appears to have gone unnoticed. The CO, therefore, had another chance of a surprise attack upon these vessels, but he made no attempt. Instead, he ordered transmission of a short sighting report by W/T at 0009, which had promptly been D/F'd by HMCS *Ottawa,* which was evidently the rear guard on our port beam. Although the bearing of 85° from her was spot on, the distance was way out; three miles would have been a more realistic estimate. However, from this information, it can be deduced that our close proximity to both these escorts and the convoy itself had still not been detected.

At 0009, the KTB also shows the CO's intentions of moving up on the convoy's moon-lee flank in order to gain a forward position and then to penetrate the convoy from the front. In actuality, he made no move toward carrying out this idea because the B-bar one hour later, at 0108, had been D/F'd by HMCS *Ottawa* at 135° from her. This meant that we were still behind the stern sweepers, and instead of moving forward, we must have fallen back somewhat. The S.O.E. likewise made no move, for in his report in regard to the D/F'd B-bar at 0108, he stated that it had been decided to wait for an hour to see if any amplifying report would be made.

A little more than twenty minutes later, at 0130, the KTB mentioned that the rear escort and the straggler had drifted astern. We are further informed that there was one destroyer covering the convoy's port side and beyond her were four largish shadows. With regard to this first statement, we do not know which of the escorts had drifted astern, or if both of them reduced their speed, or if one merely kept her station. If both had conveniently dropped back without even spotting us as they drifted by, the boat would have had a clear run to the convoy because the rearmost merchantman was about 3-4 miles ahead of us. The CO did not make any such run. The second statement would have us believe that he was to port of the destroyer covering the convoy's port side, at this point. If this were correct, he could not have possibly seen four largish shadows beyond her. The distance to the flank escort was given as 6,000 metres, and she was some 5,000 yards to port of the convoy. The distance from the boat to the convoy was, therefore, in the region of 11,000 metres. However, the horizon, as seen from the bridge of a U-boat in daylight and good visibility, would at best be about 8,000 to 9,000 metres; at night, this distance would be greatly reduced. Therefore, it was not possible for the CO to view those largish shadows at night because of the distance, as well as the darkness.

Returning to the escorts dropping back, it follows that it must have been HMCS *Ottawa* which had drifted astern, thus leaving a gap where the boat could have slipped through and across HMCS *Ottawa's* path to reach its stated position–totally unobserved. This was actually quite remarkable. HMCS *Ottawa* had D/F'd the boat's transmissions twice within one hour and, although its position had not been determined, she, as well as HMCS *Dunver* were then aware that a U-boat was on their tail somewhere; therefore, increased vigilance would surely have been a matter of urgency. Yet, this boat was moving about in close proximity to, and crossing the path of, HMCS *Ottawa* without being spotted at all. This does not seem very likely, considering the situation. However, if such a maneuver was successful, it would pose yet another question: Why and how did the CO take the boat to the port side of the flank escort, when he had the opportunity of remaining inside the screen? After all, HMCS *Ottawa* had drifted astern (or so we are led to believe), thereby giving him ample space to slip through, and he could thus have sneaked up toward the convoy unopposed, keeping the flank escort to port and having the convoy unprotected on the starboard side of the boat. This should have been the actions of any competent CO.

At 0147, apart from being (allegedly) athwart the convoy, the KTB also tells us that the port side destroyer was turning toward the boat at zero inclination, that the CO ran off at full speed, and that the destroyer presented herself in a broadside-on inclination every quarter of an hour.

Obviously, the CO should have attacked, beginning with the flank escort in particular, because she so obligingly presented her broadside every fifteen minutes, and therefore, should not have been missed. This attack should have been followed by going after the convoy, and finishing with an unobstructed escape at maximum speed until diving out of sight and ultimately obtaining success.

He did not do, nor could he have done, any of the preceding actions because his whole story, as recorded in his KTB, is false.

He could never have been athwart the convoy, encountered the flank escort on its port side, nor have been chased away by her because twenty minutes after these KTB entries, our B-bar at 0208 had been D/F'd once again by HMCS *Ottawa* in 125° from her. Of even greater significance is the fact that HMCS *Dunver*, on our starboard side, obtained a radar contact at the very same time, placing us in 100° true, at a distance of 3.5 miles. In other words, HMCS *Ottawa's* D/F-bearing and HMCS *Dunver's* radar fix provided a perfect cross-bearing of our position, and that proved that we were still *behind* the convoy and between the two stern sweepers. The same place, in fact, that we had been for two hours. Neither of them had drifted astern, and the boat could not have possibly been athwart the convoy some twenty minutes before transmission of the B-bar. Fortunately for us, HMCS *Dunver's* radar fix had been discounted as being a false alarm, and the escorts still did not know where, exactly, the boat was located.

From this, it follows that the KTB entries of 0130 and 0147 are blatantly false. For example, how many quarter hours are there in twenty minutes? The contents of the B-bar 0208 are false as well, because it stated that he was being forced away by a destroyer. The KTB implies that this was the flank escort, which, realistically, we could not have been anywhere near. If, on the other hand, we were to assume that he had been athwart the convoy and that this escort had been forcing him away, she would have, undoubtedly, alerted HMCS *Ottawa*, who would have joined in and blocked our path. This would have also sealed the boat's fate because we would have been caught on the surface between the two.

It would have also been impossible for the boat to have reoccupied its previous position, as D/F'd by HMCS *Ottawa* and radar fixed by HMCS *Dunver* at 0208, by running at full speed. Full speed would have produced a white foaming bow-wave and an equally conspicuous wake, especially on a calm, dark sea. If their lookouts could not have spotted us under those conditions, they would have had to have been sleeping!

Neither HMCS *Ottawa* nor HMCS *Dunver* could have possibly forced us away because they picked up three of our transmissions within two hours and would have known that there was a U-boat in the vicinity; but, they had not yet pin-pointed the boat's location. Besides, when the B-bar at 0108 had been D/F'd by HMCS *Ottawa*, the S.O.E. decided to wait for one hour, which meant that there would be no action for the following sixty minutes. Yet, the B-bar at 0208, transmitted exactly one hour after the previous one, stated that he was being forced away even *before* any action had been taken. The order to HMCS *Dunver*, to search to a depth of 15 miles, had not been given until 0222, which was fourteen minutes *after* the B-bar had been sent. It follows, therefore, that no escort had forced the boat away (they did not know where we were), the contents of the B-bar was false (the CO merely used it as a cover), and the story told, from 0009, had absolutely no substance.

However, interestingly enough, the CO was not yet finished. He could not have possibly permitted himself to be exposed to an accusation of incompetence. Therefore, he continued his false entries with 0245, which stated that the destroyer was out of sight and that he was operating upon the convoy's course. In order to understand what he was saying at that point, one must look at the position of the convoy. The story, according to his KTB and illustrated in Chart 2 simply does not add up.

At 0800 on 3 February, the convoy was in AM 7196, traveling at about 7 knots on a heading of 220° true. The boat was being overrun by its port wing in AL 9955 at 2300, and was in AL 9957 at 0000 of the fourth, when the CO reported the sighting of same with a W/T at 0009 right on the convoy's tail. The S.O.E. assumed this W/T to be a report on a straggler, for this transmission was, at that stage, placed at over 30 miles away. The next sighting signal by B-bar 0108, had correctly been taken as such, and it must be assumed that the convoy changed its course by 15° as a precautionary measure shortly thereafter; for when the following B-bar of 0208 was D/F'd, the S.O.E. stated that the convoy was steering 235° and traveling at 9 knots. This obviously exposes the inaccuracy of the KTB entry.

The port wing of ON-222 was, therefore, in AL 9974 (with the boat on its tail), instead of having turned due south, being in AL 9978 and heading for BE 2315, as per the KTB. At the same time, the S.O.E. had ordered the three vessels of the Escort Group to sweep down the port side of the convoy in search of the U-boat, and if, as we are induced to believe, U-764 was racing up the convoy's port side to get in front of same, the boat would be running right into the guns of the Escort Group, thus leaving it hopelessly trapped.

Thus, even if the CO had attempted to carry out his stated intention of reaching the convoy's forward sector, he would have never made it. And, as Chart 3 shows, it was he who turned onto a course of about 180° and not the convoy. If he was in BE 2314 at 0400, as stated in the KTB, that would have been the only course to get him there. Furthermore, while he was moving away from the convoy, he did not make another report, in spite of having been ordered to do so by W/T 0250 of the fourth.

At 0407, the KTB implies that the boat was in front of and on the starboard side of the convoy, whereas Chart 3 illustrates this to be false. If his statement were correct, he would have had to have been in AL 9894 or AL 9886, but he was some thirty miles to the southeast of that position in BE 2314. In an attempt at making his story ring true, he finally reported, by W/T 0500, that the convoy was in BE 2315. Its correct position, however, at that time would stretch from about AL 9897 to BE 2231, which is some 20-25 miles west-northwest of the boat's position. This estimate of the distance between boat and convoy depends, of course, upon whether the boat's position, as per KTB, was correct in the first place. This, however, may not be the case at all, because HMCS *Ottawa* had picked up yet another Enigma message at 0531 on a bearing of 91° from her.

If this was our W/T 0500 which, as per KTB had been transmitted at 0532, then we could not have possibly been in BE 2314, but would still have been trailing behind the convoy in about AL 9898. On the other hand, HMCS *Ottawa* may have been dealing with a transmission from another boat while ours went out a minute later and may have been missed, for once. Whatever the case may have been the position of ON-222, as reported in W/T 0500, is false.

As already mentioned previously, this CO could, and did, make up nearly any story he wished without harbouring the slightest apprehension of being discovered. Today, however, we have access to the British records, and the facts contained therein provide conclusive evidence of the false entries made by this man in his KTB. If further proof be required, OL Boddenberg, the CO of U-963, unwittingly supplied more by his B-bar at 0811 on 4 February and by his subsequent W/T 0842. Although the contents of the B-bar was complete nonsense, its transmission, nevertheless, revealed his position, which had again been accurately D/F'd by HMCS *Ottawa*. OL Boddenberg reported having fired four single torpedoes at a southwest bound convoy in BE 2225 at 0750. Though the range was only 5-7 hectometres, he achieved no success, and air and surface units forced him to go below. The convoy's position, at 0820, was given as BE 2227, steering a course of 240° true.

There cannot be the slightest doubt as to the identity of this convoy, as the stated times, courses, and positions point directly to where ON-222 was at that time which contrasts the twenty some miles to the east, as per U-764's KTB. Although Bremen received praise from Rear-Admiral Godt, the Chief of Operations, for his "attacking spirit" which was induced by his false entries in his KTB, he had, in fact, done nothing at all. It also appears that OL Boddenberg was overlooked and not recognized for actually going on with the attack of this same convoy.

In this context, it may be illuminating to compare this CO's inaction with the actions of another competent one, who was indeed reliable for attacking at the right time. This is related in W/T 1931 of 4 March 1944, in which HQ transmitted an *admonitory message* stating that

> KL Mannesmann, the CO of U-545 (a IXc boat), had picked up hydrophone bearings of a convoy in the daytime. He made a submerged high speed run, lasting about an hour, managed to penetrate the protecting screen, and went right into the convoy unobserved. There he sunk three steamers and torpedoed a fourth. The two remaining T5s were intended to be used against the escorting destroyers, and with this in mind, he remained at twelve metres, raised the big periscope, while still inside the convoy, and waited until being noticed by some of the escorts. The destroyers, however, contrary to the CO's expectations, did not close in to attack, but circled the boat hesitatingly until, suddenly, they made off at high speed. There were no countermeasures.

Before closing this chapter, one should also consider some of the orders applying to the situation on ON-222, as given in the *Handbook for U-Boat Commanders*, a copy of which is issued to every CO. Some examples of these orders are as follows:

> ...A U-boat's weak points must be overcome and counterbalanced by skillful handling in a tactical manner, by operating to the fullest extent and by taking advantage of even the slightest chances of success, exploiting those with tenacity...
>
> ...the object of the submerged attack is to fire with accuracy at short range and to remain unobserved while doing so. Relevant data as to the enemy's course, speed, distance, etc. will increase in accuracy as the range shortens...
>
> ...at dusk and on clear moon-lit nights submerged attacks can also be mounted, but care must be taken under such conditions as the U-boat may be much closer to the enemy than had been thought. The U-boat must exploit the rare opportunity of attacking an enemy by using all its torpedoes and by accepting any risk to itself, irrespective of how extensive the enemy's patrol activities may be...
>
> ...the possibilities offered by the fire control station should be used to their fullest advantage, so that, having reached a favourable position for an attack on a convoy or a number of ships, the situation can be exploited by firing multiple shots immediately at several targets. No reliance can be placed upon any favorable attacking position presenting itself again...
>
> ...the purpose of surface attack is to fire torpedoes at short range and to remain unobserved; such attack, therefore, is only carried out at night...
>
> ...as soon as the first target has been attacked, further attacks should be made upon a second and a third. This will be easier after the first explosion on account of the confusion arising amongst the enemy at night...
>
> ...every chance should be taken to destroy the troublesome sweepers of the enemy's escorts, as it is in the interest of all U-boats in the vicinity that the number of destroyers, corvettes etc. be reduced during the preparation of an attack upon the convoy...

> ...only by fighting spirit, instant decision making, independent actions, resolute persistence, solid skill and by directing other U-boats to the target even after one's own attack, will success be achieved...
>
> ...during collective operations of U-boats, no distinction can be made between reconnaissance and attack. If only one of these commitments can be executed, attack must always have complete priority!

Although KTB entries imply that these orders had been followed and obeyed, the facts clearly prove otherwise.

Conclusion

The concern, at this point, is not whether the CO does or does not attack, damage, or sink any vessel because the presence of a convoy, or any other target, is merely a circumstance that permits seeing this man in his true colors. Evidence has proven that he revealed both incompetence and disobedience of the orders and directives issued by HQ in relation to such actions. The object of this book is to illustrate the CO's concealment of his actions by falsities and omissions in his KTB. In short, he had the best opportunity for action that any CO could have wished for. Without effort on his own part, he found himself undetected and surrounded by various targets; however, there was no action pursued.

Having surfaced behind the convoy, still undetected, the only action taken during the following two hours was the orders for three transmissions by means of which he made our presence known. Apart from that, he simply loitered about, behind the targets, until turning away to port and then diving out of sight and leaving the actual attack to other boats. Of course, none of this could be revealed to HQ, therefore, he took recourse to falsification, for he knew that the danger of his actions being exposed at that time was virtually nonexistent.

Both OL Boddenberg and KL Mannesmann displayed competence and attacking spirit, and they went into action first and transmitted the results thereafter, as per the directives given in the *Handbook*. However, Bremen chose to do things his own way, regardless, and he continued doing so with impunity.

Chapter Three

Convoy or No Convoy

Although OL Boddenberg in U-963 attacked ON-222 from close range (thus following the orders of the handbook), every "fish" failed to find its target, and the convoy continued its journey in a west-southwesterly direction toward its destination without suffering any loss. U-764, on the other hand, had withdrawn, turned north, and was at 0800, on a heading of 358° true.

As per KTB entries 4-2-44

The boat was at 0800 in BE 2314, had moved to BE 2311 at 1200, at 1600 we were in AL 9978 and at 2000 had reached AL 9971. Four hours later, at 0000 on 5 February, the boat was alleged to be in AL 9477 and at 0400 its position was given as AL 9563.

Facts

AL 9978 cannot be reached from BE 2311 on a course of 358° true. AL 9477 is more than one hundred miles from AL 9971, and to reach the former in four hours would require a speed in excess of 24 knots, which a VIIc boats is incapable of achieving. In addition, the course to that position would be 292° true, and not 358° as stated here.

Another four hours later, at 0400, the KTB states that the boat had traveled a further one hundred miles or more, to find itself in AL 9563, which is totally out of the question. These entries are, therefore, false.

Comment/explanation

If anyone should now want to put this down to error, claiming the position given at 0000 on the fifth should have been AL 9677, then, as indicated earlier, there are obviously far too many errors in the KTB to deem it acceptable as the truth. Besides, each KTB bears the signature of the CO, therefore, he is responsible for its contents, be it error, omission, or deliberate falsification.

Eventually, on 10 February, at 0000, we had arrived in AM 4441. At 0400 the boat was in AL 6683, back to AM 4441 by 0800, still there at 1200, had moved to AL 6666 at 1600, to AL 6925 at 2000 and then, steering a course of 309° true, arrived in AL 6595 at 0000 of the eleventh. However, with W/Ts 1353 and 1504 of the tenth, received at 1845, 14 U-boats had been ordered to take up new patrol positions; ours was to be AL 6145. These W/Ts also stated that on or about the sixteenth an operation against an America-England convoy was being planned, which was intended to be assisted by our own air reconnaissance.

At around 2100 on 11 February, while keeping watch on our allotted frequency with one ear, I used the other for monitoring various different ones, as was my wont. On this occasion, I picked up R/T-traffic from a convoy on 2410 Kc/s = 124.5 m. After reporting this to the CO in the control room, I asked permission for extending the D/F-loop in order to take a bearing. Brusquely he snapped that I could not possibly have heard any R/T-traffic from a convoy in that area. He then denied my request for the extension of the D/F-loop.

As per KTB entries 11-2-44

At 1600, the boat was in AL 6197 and surfaced at 1941, steering 40° true. At 2000, in AL 6194, the weather was described as bad, with winds from west-northwest at force 7, the sea was running at force 6, plus mist and bad visibility. Swamping breakers were said to render observations by the lookouts on the bridge extremely difficult. Some two hours later, the boat was ordered below to a depth of fifty metres and was then steering 270° true.

Facts

First of all, there is yet another error in these KTB entries because the wind was not from the west-northwest, but from the west-*south*west. There is no entry as to the R/T-traffic reported to the CO, nor of his refusal to permit a bearing to be taken. Assistance for locating the convoys had been provided by equipping the boats with a receiver that had a frequency range which included that of the convoy R/T. Coupling said receiver to the D/F-loop permitted bearings to be obtained.

The CO of U-764, however, had no intention of taking advantage of this assistance by either allowing himself to be guided to the convoy, or, at least, reporting its presence and direction to HQ. He supplies the truth thereof himself by 1) dismissing my report out of hand, without even taking the time to listen to the traffic himself; 2) preventing a bearing to be taken; 3) concealing these facts by making no entry of same in the KTB; 4) striking out that portion of my radio report where date and time of said R/T-traffic had been mentioned, and ordering me to write same again, but omitting any reference to those facts.

Apart from that, his outright denial of the presence of a convoy is also false, as there was, in fact, an east-bound convoy in that area at the date and time in question, steering about 65° true.

According to British records (ADM 199/1337), this convoy was SC-152, sailing on 29 January from Halifax with thirty ships, including twelve tankers, and arriving in the UK on 15 February without loss.

Ocean Escort	1 Destroyer	:	*Hotspur*
	2 Corvettes	:	*Nasturtium, Woodstock*
Group C4	1Frigate	:	*Curzon*
	2 Corvettes	:	*Trillium, Brandon*
	1 MAC	:	*Acavus*
Support Group B1	2 Destroyers	:	*Watchman, Wanderer*
	2 Corvettes	:	*Strule, Bryon*

Position of this convoy at 0800 GMT on:

10 February = AK 9992 (51:14N X 26:43W)
11 February = AL 8132 (53:37N X 22:11W)
12 February = AM 6645 (55:00N X 17:17W)
13 February = AM 4632 (55:28N X 11:43W)
Average speed was 7 1/2 knots.

The ships were proceeding in columns at five cables apart and the ships in column were at three cables distance. The weather was very bad, mostly gales from the south, and there were many breakdowns.

At the time in question, approximately between 2000-2400 on 11 February, boat and convoy would be roughly 60 miles apart (see Chart 4 and Chart 1), and the bad weather, coupled with those many breakdowns, made the use of R/T inevitable. This was the traffic I had picked

Chart Four

63
66
69
2000
10 Feb
0800
12 Feb
62
65
68
0800
11 Feb
2000
11 Feb
0800
12 Feb
2100
11 Feb
61
64
67
A
L
2000
12 Feb
0800
13 Feb
52
55
58

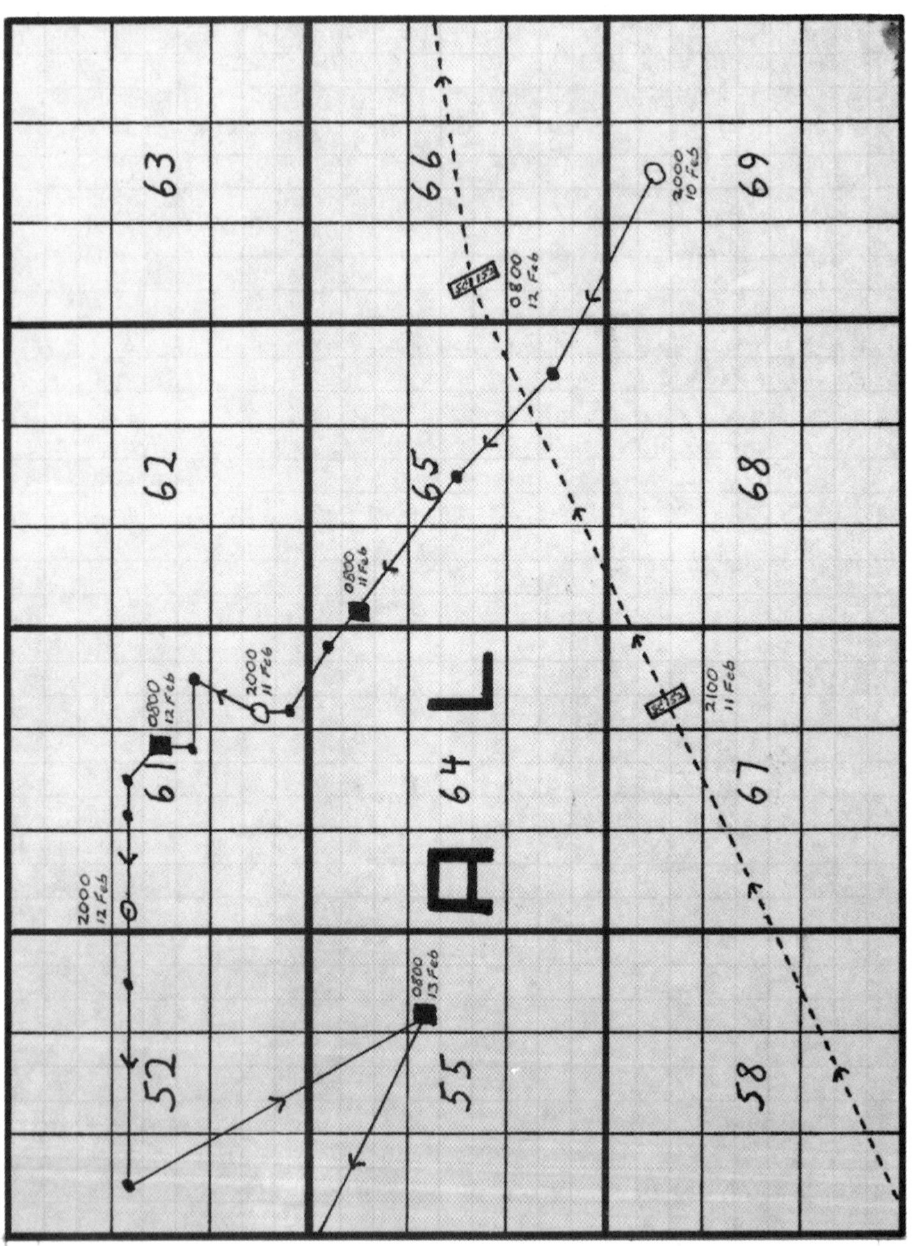

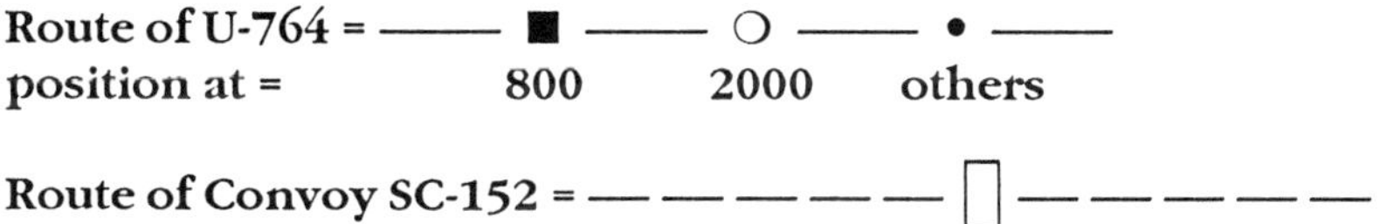

At the time in question, about 2100 on 11 February 1944, boat and convoy were, roughly, 60 miles apart, and the R/T-traffic from the convoy could be received without any problem—as, in fact, was the case.

up, and neither the omission by the CO, nor the ordered falsification of my radio report can alter that fact.

Tests had been established that R/T-traffic could be received from distances of up to 300 miles, and bearings had been obtained when traffic was D/F'd at about 60 miles.

Comment/explanation

It is obvious that the CO had no intention of attacking this or any other convoy, as had already been revealed a week previously. We were being overrun by part of ON-222, the engine and propeller noises of the vessels passing overhead had been heard by the entire crew. That meant that he could not conceal the presence of that convoy, and he had to do something.

Having failed to mount a submerged attack upon the lead destroyers on approach, or upon the merchantmen while among them, he surfaced and found himself between two of the rear escorts. Although having all the data required plus good visibility, he did not even attempt a surface attack on those escorts either. According to the KTB, he intended to go in from the front (where he had been already), then he wanted to penetrate from the rear again, and finally, he decided to wait. He also went down, up, and down again until it was too late to do anything at all; boat and convoy parted company in different directions.

On this occasion, however, no such *performance* was necessary in order to preclude any direct or indirect contact with SC-152. The crew, as a whole, had no knowledge of the convoy's existence or proximity, the control room personnel within ear-shot (when I reported to the CO) had been sidetracked by his retort, and HQ was, therefore, kept in complete ignorance. If he had not forestalled the taking of a bearing, he would have been obliged to enter same in the KTB and to send a signal of the relevant data to HQ. The consequence of this would have been an order to either close this convoy for an attack, or to act as contact-keeper by shadowing same and transmitting D/F-signals for other boats, in order for them to organize a combined attack.

By the simple but most effective action of blocking the use of the direction finder, he circumvented any risks, and the KTB omission plus the fraudulently ordered falsification of my radio report served to keep HQ totally in the dark, and himself thoroughly covered.

Upon handing in and discussing the radio report with the Flotilla Communications Officer, I drew his attention to these events and mentioned that part of the report had been falsely entered by order of the CO. Although he accepted my statement and explanation, he pointed out that the CO had signed the report and that there was nothing anyone could do to cast doubt upon it. In other words, the man wearing the white cap was free to do whatever suited his own purpose without incurring the risk of being answerable for his actions. Each and every report had to be signed by him, and anything bearing his signature was intended to be accepted without question from above, while it was unassailable from below.

In this context, the reader should be reminded of the KTB entry of 0245 on 4 February. In this entry, the CO stated that there was no minimum obtainable on the D/F-frequency; whereas, the direction finder had not been used at all, as there was no need for so doing. In this case, however, the use of D/F was paramount for obtaining a bearing on this convoy. Not only did he prevent such action to be taken, he denied the very presence of the convoy by both omission in the KTB and by the order to falsify the radio report accordingly.

The orders covering this situation may also be found in the *Handbook for U-Boat Commanders* under the heading "Contact-Keeping with a Convoy." These guidelines state the following:

> ...Once an enemy convoy has been located, continued attacking is the most important task of a U-boat. If the boat is driven off or forced below by the escorts, it must not succumb to intimidation, but must try to renew contact by steering in the direction of the enemy's mean course and then attack again. No attention is to be paid to fuel consumption while keeping contact and during attacks upon a convoy, provided the tanks hold sufficient fuel for the boat's return to base...
>
> ...a U-boat, even before attacking itself, must report the sighting of a convoy or any other important target immediately, in particular if additional boats are intended to join in the attack. The sighting boat must continue signaling, even during its own attacks, so that contact is being maintained...
>
> ...Every U-boat has to consider its own attack first of all, and attack, unless receiving orders to the contrary, has to be given absolute priority. However, if a boat has been ordered to act as contact-keeper, it can only go to the attack on the orders of Operational Control. If a boat does intend to attack, it must inform all other boats of this decision by transmitting the relevant short-signal...
>
> ...The enemy may be put on guard by W/T-transmissions, but whatever disadvantage may arise therefrom must be weighed against the lack of information for other U Boats; as they will be unable to reach the target. Transmission in this case is more important than radio silence...
>
> ...Apart from signaling details of a boat's intentions to attack, accurate and regular reports of any contact made are to be transmitted every hour by the first two U-boats acting as shadowers...
>
> ...In the event of no contact report being transmitted by those shadowers, any other boats in the vicinity are to transmit once only, by short-signal, that contact had been lost. If more than 90 minutes have passed since the shadower's last report, another boat has to take over at once, on

its own initiative, instead of waiting for special orders...

...If contact has been lost by the shadower, he is to report the target's last position, course, and speed as soon as possible, and whenever contact has been lost by the other boats, through whatever cause, they must report their own position as well...

...Shadowing U-boats must shape their operation as would be most advantageous to their own attack and they must not try for better data by approaching too near the enemy when attempting to reach a forward sector, lest they jeopardize their own chances...

...The approach to the target by other U-boats in the vicinity will be greatly assisted by the shadower's D/F-signals. These are to be transmitted either by order of the Operational Control, or upon request by those other boats. They may even be transmitted upon the shadower's own initiative, if neither an order nor a request for so doing had been received in time, and if such transmissions are thought to be useful...

...If the CO should decide to transmit D/F-signals of his own accord, this must be done every half-hour on a fixed long wave in the prescribed manner, and this must be made known to the other U-boats beforehand by the appropriate W/T-message...

...In addition to other tactical considerations, absolute faultless steering of all U-boats taking part in a combined operation is of the utmost importance. This applies in particular to the boat that has made the original contact. The CO in the operational area is duty-bound to avail himself of all possible means in order to always navigate with the greatest precision. In order to achieve perfection, the boat's position should be estimated several times per day, if at all possible; and by cultivating this habit, a feel for loss of speed and of drift will be acquired...

...The shadower's report must be corrected immediately should any positional error be found therein, and if other boats discover the shadower's error, they must act likewise.

These orders apply as much to the presence of this convoy as to that of ON-222 in the previous chapter. On neither occasion did this CO obey the orders or follow the instructions given, and he concealed his disobedience by falsification of the KTB in the first case, and by omitting the relevant entries, plus ordering falsification of the radio report in this instance.

True, he reported the presence of ON-222 at both 0009 and at 0108, but the signal at 0208, stating that he had been forced away, gave no position. Had he done so and given his position correctly, he would have revealed that the convoy was not where he made it appear, and that he was, in fact, still at its tail, instead of having moved up in order to reach a forward sector.

In spite of having been ordered to report continuously, he did not do so. It was not until more than three hours later, at 0532, that he reported again. However, as we have seen, the convoy's position, as given in W/T 0500 on 4 February, was false. Moreover, this cannot be ascribed to a navigational error!

Conclusion

Having found himself in a situation over which he had little, if any, control (being overrun by ON-222) and having neatly extricated himself from this situation without taking any positive action, the CO did not intend to become involved with another convoy so soon, either as contact-keeper or attacker. He avoided this problem by simply denying the very existence of SC-152 in the first instance. This he followed up by omitting any reference to its R/T-traffic and his refusal of allowing a bearing to be taken from his KTB, and covered these omissions by ordering falsification of the radio report by deletion of the relevant entries.

A typical convoy at sea. (courtesy of IWM)

Chapter Four

There Goes Number Three

For the second time in the span of a week, both the hunter and the hunted had passed each other in the night and continued in' their respective journeys in opposite directions. The convoy, unaware of the boat's presence, maintained its easterly heading toward the UK, whereas the boat's CO, deliberately ignoring both its presence and proximity, first headed to the north, then went west, then north again, until by noon of the twelfth, he finally settled on a course of 270° true.

At 2000 on that day, he stated that he had reached the ordered position of AL 6145, whereas the one given in the KTB at that time was AL 6141. This is of no great relevance but at 1600, we were in AL 6151, and that represents submerged travel at approximately 4-5 knots for the last four hours; that was hardly in accord with the order "economical speed," as per W/T 1353 of 10 February. Perhaps, however, this KTB entry is another mistake.

At 2223 on the twelfth, W/T 1506 ordered the boats of *Group Igel 1 & 2* to move their positions 150 miles farther to the west, and the KTB states that he was heading toward the new position in AL 4241 on a course of 270° true.

On the thirteenth, at 0400, we were in AL 5242, but four hours later found the boat about 60 miles southeast of that position, in AL 5561. At 1200, however, the position was given as AL 5153. This meant that we had covered more than 75 miles in four hours. Our speed, therefore would have had to have been some 18 knots, which, even on the surface, was quite impossible.

By noon on the fourteenth, we had reached AL 4241 and HQ was in the process of activating the previously indicated convoy operation.

As per KTB entries 14/15/16-2-44

At 1200, the boat was in AL 4241, and just over two hours later, at 1415, W/T 0945 had been received, ordering *Group Igel 1 & 2* to proceed submerged in the direction of AM 53. Although the CO stated that this order was being carried out on a course of 90° true, we were still in the same square at 1600.

We surfaced at 2000 in AL 4242, and were informed by W/T 1950, received half an hour later, that one of our reconnaissance aircraft had sighted a convoy at 1800 in AM 5426, steering a course of 260° true. *Group Igel* was ordered to proceed at best speed, weather permitting, to AL 47 & 48.

The next entry states that this order was being carried out and that the boat was steering a course to the south.

At 0000 on the fifteenth, we were in AL 4281, at 0400 in AL 4561, had reached AL 4836 at 0800, dived some fifty minutes later and continued submerged at fifty metres on a course of 270° true.

The position at 1200 is given as AL 4862 and four hours later we were in AL 4861. We surfaced at 1955 in AL 5449 and we are told that there had been a drift of 82 miles in the direction of 70°, while wind and sea were from the west-by-south at force 5-6.

At 2050, the W/T 1931 ordered *Group Igel 1* to continue with all speed toward square BE 14, and the CO stated that he was running at full ahead on a course of 192° true.

W/T 2103, received at 2147, stated to *Group Igel* that a reconnaissance aircraft had sighted a convoy at 1730 in AL 4599, steering 230° true and traveling at 5 knots. HQ added that operations upon this convoy were not likely to be commenced before the evening of 18 February.

On the sixteenth at 0000, the boat was in AL 5798 and moved via AL 8423 to AL 8486 by 0800. Wind and sea had not changed, in neither direction nor force, but when diving at 0855, the boat was said to have drifted 17 miles in the direction of 170°.

Midday found us in AL 8725, 1600 in AL 8728, and four hours thereafter we were still in the same position, where we surfaced twelve minutes later.

At 2048, W/T 1913 told *Group Ige*l that the convoy had been spotted again at 1610 in AM 7416. Its speed was then 6-6.5 knots, but the course of 180°, as reported by the aircraft, was presumed to be a feint. There would be further reconnaissance during the daylight hours of the following day.

Facts

Comparing some of the positions given in the KTB (plotted in Chart 5) with both the courses steered and the drifts stated, we find that they do not match.

On 15 February at 0800, for example, we are told that the boat was in AL 4836, dived at 0851, then proceeded on a course of 270° true and arrived in AL 4862 at 1200. It is impossible to deduce how the CO arrived at this location by steering 270° true. This course, however, would be the correct one for reaching the next position in AL 4861 at 1600, but four hours thereafter the boat is said to be in AL 5449, and there had allegedly been a drift of 82 miles in 70°.

The distance from AL 4861 to AL 5449 is approximately 55 miles and the true course to arrive at that location would be approximately 37° true, with wind and sea running at force 5-6 from west by south. It is not possible for the vessel to have drifted 82 miles in 70° submerged, while arriving four hours later 55 miles away from its previous position, which had now been left behind in about 217° true.

Having arrived in AL 5449 at 2000, *Group Igel* was then ordered to go at full speed in the direction of square BE 14. In this instance, he stated that he was going full ahead, steering 192° true, and this course would indeed get him to BE 14. However, that was not where he was going. He arrived at 0000 on the sixteenth in AL 5798 instead, and the course to that position would be about 156° true.

From position AL 5798, he does appear to be on a heading to 192° true, for at 0400 he was in AL 8423. However, instead of maintaining this course, he appears to have changed to 180° true because at 0800 the boat was in AL 8486. An hour later, the KTB tells us that the boat had been subjected to drift again. This drift was stated to be 17 miles in 170°, although the direction of both wind and sea was the same and its force had actually decreased slightly.

Comment/explanation

Navigation is not my province, but taking due note of the data entered in the KTB, it would appear that the CO may have derived some benefit by taking a course in this branch. As we have seen, his KTB entries do not add up. Either some of the positions given or some of the courses stated are false, and there does not seem to be any reason for it, at least not at this stage. Once again, whether the events were falsely entered or merely errors in the recording of the data, the CO remains liable for everything written in his KTB.

Similarly, we should not overlook the fact of his diligent examination of my radio reports. When he found the entries relating to the R/T-traffic of convoy SC-152, he realized that they would expose his omission of these matters from the KTB, as well as reveal his disobedience in regard to the orders given thereto in the handbook. He, therefore, ordered the deletion of the entries in question, lest he be discovered. It follows that he should have employed equal diligence when writing his own KTB and should have scrutinized the typed copies before signing them.

Nothing of any significance happened up to late in the afternoon of the following day. At that point, the airwaves became very active with the orders for a forthcoming operation.

As per KTB entries 17/18-2-44

At 1600 of the seventeenth, the boat is stated to have been in BE 1456, and little more than two hours later, W/T 1620 ordered *Group Igel* to remain at reception depth for VLF transmissions.

W/T 1633 followed at 1937, which advised *Group Igel* that the convoy had been sighted an hour earlier in AL 8912, steering a course of 270° true. *Igel* was ordered not to cross the southern boundary of the large square AL.

U-764 was at 1945 on a course of 340° true, and ten minutes later, the W/T 1853 followed by W/T 1941 were entered. These were again addressed to *Group Igel*, but stated that this group was being reformed into *Group Hai 1 & 2.*

Group Hai 1 was ordered to form a patrol line stretching from AL 7464 via BD 3369 to BE 1818 and this line was to be established by 1800 on 18 February. The boats detailed to this group were under the command of Hartman, Just, Ney, Krankenhagen, Kessler, Rodler, Dieterichs, Ites, Bremen, Vogler, Blauert, Brauel, Lueders, Reisener, Hungerhausen, Bertelsmann, Albrecht, Lamby, and Looks.

The boats commanded by Barleben, Boddenberg, Davidson, Luessow, Witzendorf, Wilberg and Wenzel were to form *Group Hai 2,* to be stationed in a line from AK 9925 to BE 1717 and this was to be accomplished also by 1800 on the eighteenth.

Both groups were to proceed submerged during daytime and W/T-reception on VLF was to be ensured. All boats were to surface at 2000. Late arrival at their patrol positions was not to be reported, but a shifting of the lines could be expected that night, after the reports of air reconnaissance had been evaluated.

At 2000, U-764 was in BE 1455 and proceeding toward square BD 33 on a heading of 334° true, and surfaced in good visibility at 2025.

From shortly after 2300 onwards, HQ transmitted three long-ish W/Ts (those of 2236, 2304, and 2348), advising the boats in both patrol lines of its intentions and issuing the relevant orders thereto.

This is to be a convoy battle in the old style, carried out with all available forces, comprising 26 U-boats and as many aircraft as can be mustered. The enemy has been sighted, consisting of 28 merchantmen, protected by a sea escort of medium strength and accompanied by an aircraft carrier.

The boats are urged to deliver the main blow during the first night, as the presence of carrier-borne planes would put operations during daylight in some doubt. A decision thereon would be made on the morning of the nineteenth.

If radar search be detected, the boats are to remain on the surface just the same, in order to reach the convoy at all events, and, having closed the target, should attempt attacking same energetically and tenaciously during the first night.

All tubes, loaded with T5s, are to be on standby for firing, and the AA-guns are to be fully manned so as to be ready for instant action. Saturation of the area with Aphrodite should be borne in mind, as the launching of many by all will confuse the enemy's air and surface defences.

Should this operation be continued in daylight, all boats—except those whose 37 mm AA-gun is defective—are ordered to remain on the surface, so as to ward off any air attacks and to split up the enemy's defences by weight of numbers.

In order to evaluate the convoy operation, detailed knowledge is necessary and any successes against aircraft are to be reported immediately. The carrier must be the prime target and for this one, too, the T5 is the best weapon.

Our own aircraft will be shadowing the convoy as from 2030 on the eighteenth and will transmit D/F-signals throughout the night. Bearings obtained by the boats are to be reported between 2045 and 2130 only, unless specifically ordered otherwise.

Shadower "C" will transmit D/F-signals, and the aircraft will drop contact-buoys, identification "2," in close proximity of the convoy. In addition, white magnesium marker, which will be alight for some time on the surface behind the convoy, will be dropped, this being signaled by the letter "L" on the D/F-frequency.

This operation has been prepared and planned for quite some time and has to be crowned by success. It is up to you to do your very best!

On the eighteenth, at 0000, U-764 was in BE 1179, moved to BE 1172 and then on to BE 1144 at 0800, where it went below at 0848.

At noon we were in BD 3339, and some two hours later, the W/T 1351 ordered both patrol lines of *Group Hai* to shift their positions 20 miles in direction of 150° by 2000.

At 1430, the boat was on a heading of 147° true, but at 1600 was still in the same square. Four hours later, however, the position was given as BE 1141, and shortly thereafter we came to the surface again. The W/T

2021 then ordered *Group Hai 1 & 2* to steer course 180° true as from 2100 and to proceed at a speed of 11 knots.

This was entered as having been carried out, and at 2115 the W/T 2045 ordered *Group Hai* to report any D/F-bearings even after 2130, until this be countermanded, thereby canceling the orders issued previously.

At 2230, W/T 2219 gave *Group Hai 1 & 2* yet another change of their course, ordering all boats to steer due east at once and to increase their speed to 13 knots. The boats were also advised that up to that time air reconnaissance had yielded no results.

Facts

Pitting 26 U-boats and all available reconnaissance aircraft against a convoy of 28 ships with a medium sea escort plus air-cover by one carrier may sound most impressive and would appear to be a formula fully assured of success. After all, on paper and in purely numerical terms (provided, of course, all the boats could be directed to the convoy more or less simultaneously) that would mean: any three boats against one escort plus the carrier, followed by one boat each against one each of the merchantmen. The combined fire-power of at least 130 torpedoes ready in their tubes plus an equal number of AA-guns simply could not fail—or could they?

The concept may have been feasible in the planning stages and in theory, but in practice the best laid plans have a habit of disintegrating either right at the beginning or at the crucial moment of execution, or all along the line, as was the case here.

There was no convoy-battle, either old-style or in any other way, and the reasons for this non-event were numerous and varied. For example:

1) The 26 U-boats ordered to take up their respective patrol positions on 17 February (as per W/Ts 1853 and 1941) were no longer available. They had been reduced to nineteen because seven of those named had already been sunk between 13 January and 11 February, although HQ may not have been aware of their loss at that time. Those seven were: KL Wenzel (U 231), sunk on 13 January; OL Barleben (U-271) and OL Luessow (U-571), sunk on 28 January; OL Blauert (U-734) on 9 February; OL Wilberg (U-666) on 10 February; OL Lueders (U-424) and OL Ney (U-283) on the following day. Thus, *Group Hai 1* had been reduced from nineteen to sixteen boats and *Group Hai 2* from seven to just three!

2) U-boat HQ had to find the convoy first, have it shadowed to determine its course, speed and daily position so as to move the patrol lines in order to intercept the convoy, and finally, have the reconnaissance planes transmit D/F-signals for the U-boats to home-in on.

During the planning stages and before commencement of these reconnaissance flights, 17 aircraft had been scheduled for this task. However, of the eleven JU-290s, only five were serviceable, the four JU-88s were ready for this operation but the two BV-222s were not; it was expected that one of those might be serviceable on the thirteenth or fourteenth. Of the twenty-four anticipated reconnaissance missions, only fourteen had actually been flown.

Nevertheless, initially the plan functioned well. The convoy had been located (in its original composition) on three successive days, the fourteenth to the sixteenth. However, two JU-290s were shot down by enemy aircraft on the sixteenth. After this, things went drastically wrong.

First, at 1530 on the seventeenth, the aircraft reported the convoy in AM 9812 on a course of 270°, whereas the correct position, at 1400, would be approximately BE 2152 and steering a course of 230° true. This represents a discrepancy in the region of 80 miles. This, of course, could be due to faulty navigation of the aircraft or a course alteration by the convoy, although there is no indication of the latter in the British records.

Second, due to engine problems, there was no reconnaissance during the daylight of the eighteenth. HQ, therefore, had no data as to the convoy's position, course, and speed, nor was the staff informed of some other far-reaching changes that had taken place since the last reconnaissance report had been received in the early afternoon of the seventeenth. Those changes will be referred to in due course. Nevertheless, HQ had not given up hope yet and planned to have two JU-290s on the convoy by 2030 for transmission of D/F-signals to the U-boats (as per W/T 2348 of the seventeenth).

In the meantime, the patrol-lines had been moved initially to the south, but when, by 2000 of the eighteenth, no aircraft reports had been received, the U-boats were ordered to steer due east. That turned out to be a very big mistake.

Comment/explanation

At this stage there is not much to be said, except perhaps, that the performance of the reconnaissance aircraft was certainly less than satisfactory. This pertains to both the number of aircraft actually available, as well as to the accuracy of their reports, more of which will be heard at a later stage.

For the moment, it may be worth pointing out that this is by no means a new problem. As far back as 1941, Doenitz had made numerous representations to his superiors with a view of having the strength of Air Group Atlantic increased. He had asked for more serviceable aircraft to fly more missions, in order that once a convoy was located, updating reports could be received at least three to four times in a twenty-four hour period, instead of having to be content with just one such report during the same time.

However, as can clearly be seen from these events, nothing had changed at all. The number of available aircraft was still as inadequate as ever, resulting in just one report per day, and, as we have seen, a wrong one at that. They had missed the real target because there was no proper continuity, they picked up and reported quite different convoys and thereby caused confusion at HQ which led to the misdirection of the patrol lines. I have no doubt that these fellows did their best under difficult circumstances, and there is no intention of even attempting to belittle the efforts of Air Group Atlantic. The blame for all these inadequacies must be laid at some other door.

U-764's KTB entry at 1937 on the seventeenth refers to the convoy being in AL 8912. Although this entry does not add to the mentioned confusion, it is false just the same because there is no such square. The correct square is AL 9812, as had, in fact, been transmitted by HQ.

Two of the circumstances contributing to the failure of this operation have already been mentioned in (1) and (2) above, but those may be described as being of a minor nature. Before considering the really crucial factors, however, the events of the following day should be viewed first.

As per KTB entries 19-2-44

At 0000, U-764 was in BE 1184, and half an hour later, the W/T 0017 advised *Group Hai* that our air reconnaissance had so far failed to locate the convoy but the search was being continued.

At 0200, the CO stated that D/F-signals were being transmitted by an aircraft, and twenty minutes thereafter, he ordered transmission of a B-bar signal, reporting his position as in BE 1195 and that the aircraft had been D/F'd in 114° true. To this entry he added that he was operating upon those D/F-signals.

The W/T 0208, entered under the time of 0245, ordered both *Hai Groups* to remain with their northern parts at their present position and to dive at daybreak.

At this time the CO stated that the operation had been discontinued.

At 0400, U-764 was in BE 1274, wind and sea were light and there was medium visibility. Twenty-two minutes later, HQ advised *Group Hai 1,* by W/T 0326, that the convoy, according to uncertain bearings at 0200, would be in an area somewhere between BE 1910 and BE 1660, proceeding at about 7 knots on an estimated course of, roughly, 210° true. The group was ordered to operate at all speed upon this data. In addition, Vogler, Blauert, Bremen and Dieterichs were specifically ordered to go for this convoy and the group was advised that further D/F-signals were to be expected.

The CO then assumed the convoy to be steering a course of 225° true, and he turned the boat onto 170° true.

Almost two hours later, the W/T 0556 told *Group Hai* that good D/F-bearings place the convoy in BE 1942 at 0500, and the group was ordered to exploit every opportunity.

At 0728, the W/T 0709 urged *Group Hai* to make fullest use of the darkness but to dive at dawn and to remain at periscope depth so that any possible chance of an attack during brightness could be seized.

U-764 was in BE 1547 at 0800 and dived at daybreak, half an hour later. Hydrophone search detected a sound source in 270° true, but this was adjudged to be one of our own boats. The periscope did not reveal anything and the sound source disappeared again.

Noon found the boat in BE 1578, and at 1330 the course was stated as 270° true.

Finally, the W/T 1255, entered at 1443, wound up the operation by disbanding *Group Hai,* and U-764 eventually moved off to the north.

Facts

Some of the inadequacies regarding this convoy operation have already been mentioned in (1) & (2) above, and now we turn to the real and weighty reasons for its complete failure.

3) This convoy was the west-bound ONS-29, sailing from the UK on 12 February and arriving at its destination, without loss, on 3 March. The intelligence and sighting reports as to the composition of the convoy had been correct originally, but a number of further vessels had joined sometime during the fourteenth, bringing the total up to forty-five. Initial protection was provided by nine escorts and two MACs, reinforced by two support groups on both the seventeenth and the eighteenth, but there had been no up-dating reports of same for the U-boats, in spite of the situation having undergone a dramatic change. This, of course, was due to the absence of any reconnaissance.

Approaching the patrol lines, the convoy's defences consisted of the following vessels:

Ocean Escort B6	3 Destroyers	:	*Fame, Vesper, Vanquisher*
	1 Frigate	:	*Deveron*
	5 Corvettes	:	*Rose, Vervain, Acanthus Eglantine, King Cup*
	2 MACs	:	*Empire Mackendrick, Alexia*
Support Group	3 Destroyers	:	*Icarus, Gatineau, Chaudiere*

18	2 Frigates	:	*Nene, Waskesieu*
Support Group	2 Frigates	:	*Rother, Wear*
10	2 Corvettes	:	*Findhorn, Lossie*
	1 Sloop	:	*Spey*

4) Considering the strength of the escort, it is obvious that the numerical balance of power had shifted heavily in favour of the convoy forces. If, again, all the U-boats were in contact with the targets at approximately the same time, there was one escort against one U-boat plus the aircraft of the two MACs. However, as the patrol lines were widely stretched and thinned out already, and HQ did not yet know when and where the convoy might cross those lines, only a handful of boats would be in the correct position to make contact; provided, of course, that the convoy should quite unsuspectingly run right into those lines. This, however, was not the case.

5) Although we did not know it at that time, it is now clear that the whole operation, irrespective of how well it may have been planned, was an open book to the other side from the start. All our W/T-traffic had not only been tapped but had been decrypted by the people at Bletchley. Our secrecy in regard to W/T-traffic, our changes of the basic settings of the cipher machine (the rotors every twenty-four hours and the plugboard connections every twelve), our efforts of ciphering anything and everything was all a complete waste of time. We could have done without the cipher machines, code books and any similar such paraphernalia, and conducted our communications in plain language from the outset because our opponents were reading at least 90 percent of our messages. Therefore, they were far better informed of the events, both actual and potential, than we were ourselves. In fact, this had been the case for some years!

The British Admiralty knew, for example, (from the W/Ts 1353 and 1504 of the tenth) which U-boats would be waiting in which positions and (from the W/Ts 1853 and 1941 of the seventeenth) any subsequent changes in the patrol lines. Appropriate counter-measures could thus be planned well in advance and put into operation by both diverting the convoy in an attempt of steering it around the patrol lines, and by reinforcing the ocean escort with the ten vessels of the two support groups during 17/18 February.

The convoy, bound for Cape Cod, was expected to steer a median course of about 250° true, but with the threat of twenty-six U-boats laying in wait across this route, a median course of approximately 225° true had been taken up until noon of the nineteenth, turning onto a westerly heading thereafter. This course would bring the convoy farther to the south, and the patrol lines would, hopefully, be evaded. It would keep

Route travelled by U-764 between 15 & 20 February 1944, as per KTB.

Position at (German time):

0800 = ——— ■ ———

2000 = ——— ❍ ———

between = ——— • ———

Convoy position (GMT):

0800 = — — — — ▮ — — — —

others = — — — — ▯ — — — —

Convoy position as given by German A/C = X

Chart Five

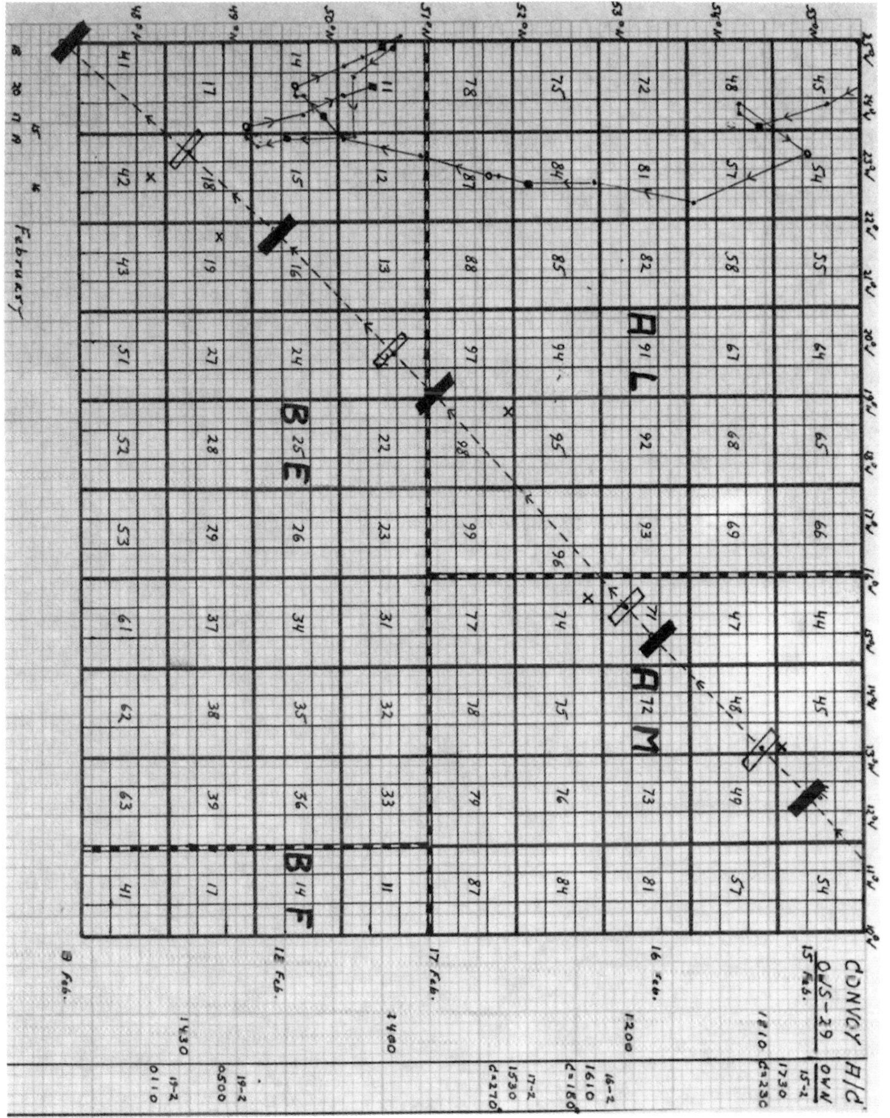

the convoy from as much danger as possible, though the crossing may be extended by an extra day, in particular in the danger zone of the eastern Atlantic.

This can be seen by the data available and illustrated in Chart 5, which shows the following positions:

14 Feb at 0800 =	AM	5165	(55:54N x 10:11W)	8 knots
15 Feb at 0800 =	AM	4658	(54:53N x 12:19W)	5.5 knots
15 Feb at 1815 =	AM	4833	(54:26N x 13:10W)	
16 Feb at 0800 =	AM	7161	(53:18N x 14:55W)	8 knots
16 Feb at 1200 =	AM	7181	(53:01N x 15:22W)	
17 Feb at 0800 =	AL	9799	(50:59N x 19:05W)	8 knots
17 Feb at 1400 =	BE	2152	(50:39N x 19:41W)	
18 Feb at 0800 =	BE	1671	(49:27N x 21:50W)	8 knots
19 Feb at 0800 =	BE	4414	(47:13N x 24:54W)	7 knots
19 Feb at 1100 =	BD	6683	(46:43N x 25:26W)	
19 Feb at 1240			turning onto 273° true	
19 Feb at 1740 =	BD	6672	(46:42N x 26:15W)	
			Course 262° true	7 knots

This diversion had been supplemented by the measures taken by the reinforced escort, and the S.O.E. in HMS *Fame* discussed with the Senior Officer of the 10th Escort Group how best to deploy the available vessels. On one hand, they had to ensure the defence of the convoy; on the other, they also wanted to take the offensive to the U-boats, for the reports of the shadowing aircraft left little doubt as to the presence of a number of U-boats lying in wait somewhere ahead in the convoy's path.

The outcome of these discussions (as reported in ADM 217/143) was the formation of a screen, four miles ahead of the convoy, by placing three corvettes from the Ocean Escort in line abreast and three miles apart in the centre. The vessels of Support Group 18 then took up station on the port wing of the convoy, four miles apart, and those of Support Group 10 had been stationed similarly on the starboard wing. The remaining units of B6-Group would protect the convoy's flanks and stern. By these dispositions, a covering front of more than 40 miles wide was achieved, and in case of any contact being made with U-boats waiting ahead of the convoy, these could immediately be hunted down by detaching support groups from either wing, while at the same time, the three corvettes in the centre would be taking up their normal close escort position by simply dropping back.

Thus covered, the convoy continued on its way, and there were no incidents during the night of 17/18 February. Likewise the morning of the eighteenth passed uneventful.

The first blood was drawn in the early afternoon of that day by the sloop HMS *Spey.* While carrying out an A/S-sweep 20 miles on the starboard bow of the convoy, she obtained and followed up an asdic contact at 1430, and attacked and destroyed U-406, KL Dieterichs' boat, in position BE 1793 (48:32N x 23:36W), but picked up forty-five of its crew.

At this point, the escorts were fully aware of our U-boats in the vicinity and both groups were hunting contacts from dusk to midnight in an area about 20 miles northwest of the convoy. And the rescue ship *Northern Pride* reported radar and/or H/F D/F contacts having been obtained by HMS *Findhorn*, HMS *Spey*, HMS *Chaudiere* and HMS *Lossie,* but none of those led to any positive results.

In order to give the convoy additional protection, two Liberator aircraft, equipped with Leigh-lights, had been provided, and one of them did pick up two of the U-boats on the surface. Although the vessels of Escort Group 10 were investigating some radar contacts in that area, aircraft and surface units did not co-operate sufficiently to obtain any success; and the second Liberator made no contact at all.

During the early hours of the nineteenth, a number of B-bar signals had been heard on both quarters and astern of the convoy, therefore attacks had been expected. On the other hand, though the U-boats did appear to be closing in, none of the signals gave evidence of any of them being within reasonable striking distance of even the support groups, not to mention the convoy itself.

The reason for all the B-bars was assumed to be either reports being made of the convoy's R/T-traffic or, much more likely, the bearings on the shadowing aircraft's transmissions of homing signals for the U-boats. In fact, HMS *Nene* reported having obtained M/F D/F bearings, between 18° and 98°, of an aircraft shadowing a convoy. These homing signals had been heard between 0410 and 0509, on a frequency of 449 kc/s and, judging by the strength of those signals, the aircraft was estimated to be shadowing at a distance of about 40 miles from the convoy concerned.

Our reconnaissance aircraft had indeed arrived in the vicinity, and the first report, at 0110 of the nineteenth, gave a convoy position in BE 4225, whereas a second report placed same in BE 1942, four hours later. Obviously, this cannot be correct, for even a mere glance at Chart 5 or Chart 6 will reveal at once that the convoy had not reversed its course and was traveling in the opposite direction, but had maintained its heading of about 230°.

It follows that neither of the positions given by the aircraft were correct, at least not for ONS-29. Also, one must remember that HMS *Spey* had sunk a U-boat (U-406) at 1430 on 18 February in about BE 1793, 20 miles on the starboard bow of ONS-29, thereby giving the correct position of the convoy at that time. Thus, it follows that the convoy had passed right through the southern arm of *Group Hai* and was well clear of the patrol line by about 2000 of the eighteenth, if not earlier.

It had been estimated that about five or six U-boats were in contact with the convoy, but only one got as far as the close screen. This one was hunted by the Norwegian corvettes *Eglantine* and *Acanthus* right through the convoy, but—though its conning tower broke surface and disappeared again—contact had been lost after some D/C-attacks. How well the support groups dealt with the U-boat threat is also shown by the sinking of a second one, (OL Albrecht, U-386) by, again, HMS *Spey*, after a protracted hunt with HMS *Lossie*. All merchantmen remained safe, and as far as could be ascertained, no torpedoes had been fired at the convoy.

As has been illustrated, the steps taken by the British Admiralty by both diverting the convoy, thus avoiding most of the U-boats drawn up in their patrol lines, and by strengthening the escorts sufficiently to counter any remaining threat, had paid off well. Consequently, ONS-29 sailed on without loss.

However, there was another factor contributing to the failure of this operation, namely, our own air reconnaissance. It is obvious that it is infinitely more simple for an aircraft to find a convoy than could be done by a U-boat, or even by a group of them. Thus, if sufficient aircraft were available and both their navigation and their reports were accurate, they would be of invaluable help to an operation such as this. On the other hand, if the required number of missions are not flown, and if the sightings reported are less than accurate or totally in error, then their involvement is, at best, quite useless. Not to mention the fact that it is capable of putting the whole operation at risk.

Since there are no indications to the contrary, HQ took it for granted that all reports pertaining to the identity of this convoy, as well as its positions, course, and speed, did refer to ONS-29. However, there was another convoy (OS-68/KMS-42 bound for Gibraltar) right behind the other one, and on the very same track. In fact, this one had to reduce speed continually to avoid running into the slower one in front of it.

The situation had been further complicated by a southwest gale and poor visibility, resulting in both convoys being scattered and even intermingling slightly during the fifteenth, as their centres were barely 8 miles apart.

It is, therefore, of importance to know which convoy had been sighted and reported, and we should also know whether the aircraft had, or had not taken any notice of the volume of ships assembled at this stage. After all, the originally reported number of twenty-eight ships had now swelled to about one hundred, and there were a total of nineteen escorts, two MACs and the two carriers HMS *Biter* and HMS *Tracker* present. This should not have gone unnoticed, and the shadowing aircraft should have spotted these facts and circumstances, but as per HQ's W/T 1950 of the fourteenth and the W/T 2103 of the fifteenth, there was nothing to indicate that this had been done, as no change at all had been reported to the U-boats.

The following day's W/T 1913 advised *Group Hai* that the convoy had been sighted at 1610 in AM 7416, steering a course of 180° true, but the fact that this course had been taken was considered to be a feint. The evidence now available proves that both the aircraft's report and HQ's inference were wrong because the aircraft had obviously picked up the false convoy. Instead of reporting the data pertaining to ONS-29, it reported those of OS-68/KMS-42; this is underlined by the course given. HQ assumed the course of 180° to be a feint by the former, whereas the latter had, in fact, turned south toward its destination of Gibraltar and may well have steered the course reported at that time.

One must also consider the question of the number of aircraft that were actually out looking for ONS-29 on 16 February. Two JU-290s were shadowing this convoy early in the morning of that day and while doing so, also detected the KMS convoy. These shadowers had, of course, been detected and both were shot down at about 1000. One was shot down by a SKUA from HMS *Biter* and the other by a shore-based Beaufighter directed by *Biter's* fighter control. Reports indicated that those two reconnaissance aircraft did detect the KMS convoy while circling ONS-29, therefore, one would have expected them to have reported the presence of either two convoys, or one that was very large. Alas, there is no evidence of this having been done.

In the meantime, ONS-29 continued on its way and had been reported by another aircraft to be in AL 9812 at 1530 on 17 February. However, this cannot be correct either, unless the positions estimated by the tracking room and the actual ones given by the Convoy-Commodore are totally false—which does not seem very likely.

In other words, it is not known what this aircraft spotted at that time, but the target was now roughly 70 miles southwest of the position reported, and HQ must have been somewhat confused as to where the convoy really was. Engine problems kept the aircraft grounded during daylight of the eighteenth, and HQ moved the patrol lines first toward the south and later due east, whereas ONS-29 continued in a southwesterly direction. The intention, following this action, was to have all available aircraft in the assumed area by dusk of that day in the hope that D/F-signals could be transmitted from about 2030 onwards. This hope had been dashed, however, because by midnight there still had been no contact with the target.

An hour later, at 0110 on the nineteenth, one of the aircraft reported the convoy to be in BE 4225, and was said to have shadowed the convoy until 0210 and to have transmitted D/F-signals from 0130 to 0210. But KL Lamby in U-437 appears to have been the only one who noticed that this position could not have possibly been correct. He was absolutely right.

Date throughout is 19 February 1944, unless otherwise stated.

Bearings on aircraft between
0200 to 0300 = ——————
0400 to 0500 = —•—•—•—•—
0500 to 0603 = • • • • • • • • • •

Position of convoy as per British records
= — — — — ▯ — — — —

Position of convoy as per German aircraft = X

U-985 at 0237 140°
U-441 at 0209 140°
A
L
78
87
88
B
E
U-989 at 0547 133°
11
12
13
U-764 at 0220 114°
U-212 at 0201 124°
U-212 at 0505 128°
U-281 at 0519 113°
14
15
16
U-256 at 0603 148°
CONVOY at 0800 18Feb.
U-91 at 0507 120°
A/C at 0500
17
18
19
CONVOY at 1430 18Feb.
U-437 at 0217 50°
U-386 at 0420 199°
U-386 at 0509 50°
CONVOY at 2000 18Feb.
A/C at 0110
CONVOY at 0100
41
42
43
CONVOY at 0500
CONVOY at 0800
B
D
66
44

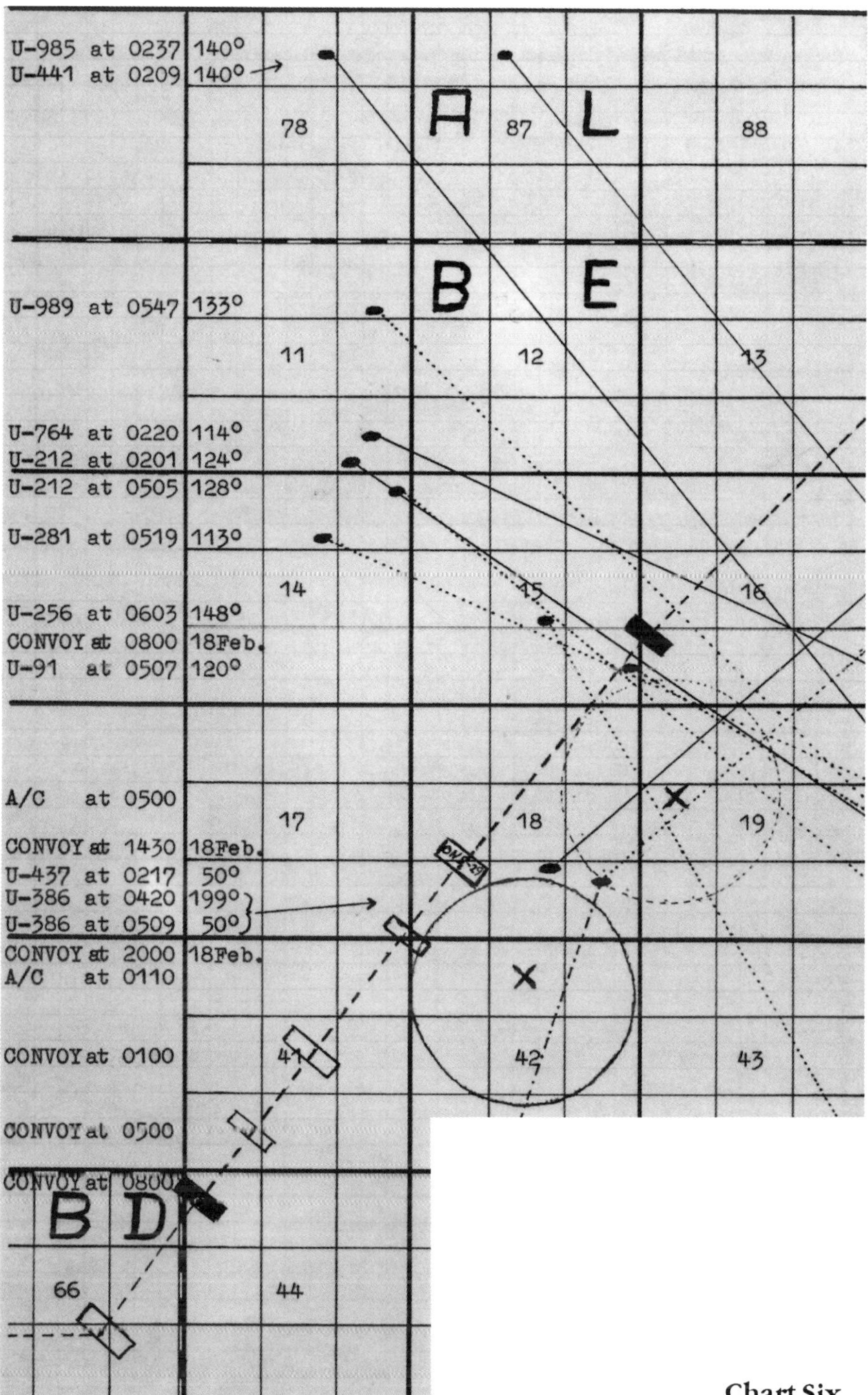

Chart Six

A glance at Chart 6 will confirm this observation because it illustrates that there was no convoy in that area (ONS-29 had already passed through the patrol line and would have been about 50 miles to the southwest of that position), and no bearings were shown to have been obtained on the aircraft, which was supposed to have been circling the convoy at the usual distance of some 40 km, while transmitting its D/F-signals.

That circle was actually, at 0420, being dissected by just one boat's bearing, U-386. However, this could not have been correct either because there was no aircraft in this position at that time. It would appear, then, that the operator in U-386 had taken the bearing on the wrong side, because if 180° is deducted from the figure given, thus placing the bearing on the right side, a reading of 19° is obtained, which has merit; a reading of 199° does not.

Up to this point, we have not yet determined what the correct position of the aircraft reporting the convoy at 0110 should have been. Likewise, we do not know whether this was the same aircraft that reported the convoy in BE 1942 four hours later, or whether there was a second one shadowing a convoy. We do know, however, that there was indeed a convoy in this area at that time, but it was not the original target. This convoy was ON-224, which was running behind on a parallel course to, but about 25 miles to the south of, the target, ONS-29. Its average speed was about two miles faster, and it was catching up with, and later overtook the ONS convoy. The distance, however, between their tracks had widened to some 45-50 miles by the night of 18/19 February.

ON-224 did, in fact, report being circled by enemy aircraft while it transmitted homing signals, and it may be helpful to first consider the bearings obtained by the U-boats which, in chronological order, are as follows:

Time of Transmission	Boat	Position	Bearing	Additional
0201	U-212	BE 1197	124°	
0209	U-441	AL 7816	140°	trans. not received
0217	U-437	BE 1883	50°	
0220	U-764	BE 1195	114°	
0237	U-985	AL 8724	140°	
0420	U-386	BE 1892	199°	wrong side
0505	U-212	BE 1433	128°	
0507	U- 91	BE 1596	120°	
0509	U-386	BE 1892	50°	
0529	U-989	BE 1138	133°	
0603	U-256	BE 1559	148°	transmission not received

Discarding the bearing of U-386 at 0420, we find that the last five bearings, between 0505 and 0603, had correctly pin-pointed the circling aircraft, thus indicating the convoy's position. There is also additional evidence as to its location: KL Looks (U-264) had been sunk by escorts of this convoy shortly after 0400 on 19 February in BE 1973; KL Lamby (U-437) was attacked by a destroyer at 0422 in BE 1952; OL Davidson (U-281) estimated the convoy's position to be approximately BE 1943 at 0500, and OL Brauel (U-256) came to the same conclusion shortly thereafter.

Incidentally, OL Brauel torpedoed HMS *Woodpecker* (one of ON-224's escorts) at 2216 on the same day in approximately BE 1853, and blew her stern off with a T5. HMS *Woodpecker* was taken in tow until deteriorating weather conditions put this salvage attempt at risk. Therefore, on the morning of the twenty-seventh, the tow was cast off and she capsized almost at once.

These facts prove that our reconnaissance had made contact with the wrong convoy, and its position, as reported at 0110, could not possibly have been correct.

Up to January 1944, the usual procedure—once the convoy had been sighted—was for the aircraft to circle the target and transmit D/F-signals at designated times and frequencies, in order to enable all U-boats in the vicinity to take bearings and transmit them, together with their own position, to HQ. The more such reports were received there, the better the chances were of calculating the convoy's position, irrespective of the original position having been given incorrectly, as was the case in this instance.

However, the situation was more complicated than it initially appeared. In a long, stretched out patrol line, only a small number of U-boats will be close enough to obtain useful bearings on the aircraft's D/F-signals and also in a position to reach the convoy, once located.

Furthermore, the aircraft will tend to stay as far away from the convoy as possible, in order to conceal the fact that it had been spotted and was being shadowed, as well as, to keep maximum distance between itself and any carrier planes. Thus, neither HQ nor any of the U-boats had an idea of where the aircraft may have been in relation to the convoy at any given time, and the position of the latter would still be subject to a certain amount of guesswork.

This can be demonstrated by means of the first five bearings from the previous table. Plotting them as per Chart 6 (solid lines), we obtain some cross-bearings, indicating the aircraft's position, but we still do not know where, exactly, the convoy is located. Taking into consideration the timings of those cross-bearings, the aircraft would appear to be flying in a straight line, on a course opposite to that of the convoy, instead of circling it. It may, of course, have reached the limit of its endurance, and while heading for its base, it did transmit some D/F-signals for the benefit of the U-boats, whereas the target was moving on.

As is evident from the above, the employment of aircraft for the location of convoys had definite merits; the procedure, however, was subject to certain limitations and imprecision. In order to overcome these problems, a small but very significant change had been devised.

Instead of the aircraft merely transmitting D/F-signals and its call sign, it was to add its own bearing to and its distance from the convoy to these transmissions. Any U-boat, having obtained a bearing on the aircraft, was then required to add the latter's data to its own and transmit the whole to HQ. By these means, the previously mentioned problems would be reduced to a minimum and HQ would obtain a far more precise location of the target than was possible hitherto, even if only one boat was in a position to transmit all the data, both its own and that of the aircraft.

This change of procedure had been announced during the first week of January 1944. I remember it very clearly, because at that time I was still working in the Flotilla Communications Office, and it was part of my duties to correct the office NBU accordingly and to ensure that all boats at the base received the new orders and corrected their NBUs as well.

Boats at sea received such corrections, or any other changes, by W/T, and the change of procedure in this case had been transmitted on all services by the W/Ts 1104 and 1137 on 22 January 1944:

> Serial No. 48 Alteration of War Order 211a
>
> In the case of transmission of beacon signals by aircraft, the new procedure will be this:
>
> A) For the purpose of sending beacon signals, the aircraft will circle the convoy on various bearings to it and at various distances as follows: After spotting the convoy, it will circle twice at intervals of about 15 minutes. Again circle twice after 30 minutes. It will then withdraw from the enemy and after about an hour will send beacon signals if flying endurance permits.
>
> B) Beacon signal "AA" with shadower's call-sign interspersed will be transmitted for about 5 minutes in each instance. Report in accordance with para. 7 of War Order 211a at the beginning and end of each transmission of beacon signals.
>
> To their reports of bearings, boats will add the corresponding report from the aircraft: bearing as 4th group, distance as 5th group of the short-signal.
>
> C) Apart from total evaluation by operational control, boats can construct geometrically a very good convoy position out of the bearings of the various transmissions in relation to their own position.

If those orders were carried out by all participants, the resulting bearing would pin-point a convoy's position very accurately. If, on the other hand, they were not obeyed, then they were worse than no bearings at all, which was the case in this instance. The difference that U-764's bearings, even if transmitted correctly, may have had on this operation, is indeterminable because too many ifs and buts would have to be considered, which would render any answer quite inconclusive. Nevertheless, when looking at the KTB entries, we find that they are not in accordance with the facts.

I obtained a bearing on the aircraft at some time between 0100 and 0130, and reported to the CO accordingly. This data should have been transmitted forthwith, but the CO gave no order for so doing. At 0200, I was relieved by PO Schulz, and while bringing him up to date as to the events that occurred during the previous six hours, I also drew his attention to the new procedure, reminding him, in particular, not to forget to include the aircraft's data, if and when the CO finally ordered a B-bar to be transmitted.

During this interchange, no D/F-signals had been received, therefore no bearing could have been taken. It follows, then, that the KTB entry at 0200, stating that "aircraft transmits D/F-signal," is false.

When I, in turn, relieved PO Schulz at 0800, I learned that a B-bar had been transmitted containing a bearing but no aircraft data. Inquiring as to the reason for this omission, he replied to the effect that the CO had expressly ordered the transmission of the bearing only. It is plainly evident that the CO deliberately ordered the wrong procedure to be used (to the contrary of the orders from HQ), and we also do not even know which bearing had actually been transmitted. It could have been the one taken roughly an hour before, which by this time would have been quite stale, useless, and even misleading; or, it may have been a fresh one which was taken after 0200, though there is no evidence of one having been obtained. There is simply no way of determining what information was transmitted.

The R/T-traffic of the convoy should also have been utilized for the determination of its position. Although one man can monitor two different frequencies at the same time (the allotted short-wave service and the D/F-frequency, for example), he cannot keep watch and take bearings on the R/T frequency as well. A competent CO, (one in possession of "attacking spirit," as according to the Chief of Operations), would have had both of us in the radio room in order to make use of anything available, including the R/T-traffic. Bremen, however, did no such thing.

Also, considering his rebuff on the eleventh (when he dismissed my report of a convoy), I did not conceive of any advantage being gained by my remaining in the radio room voluntarily, monitoring the convoy's R/T-traffic and then, more likely than not, again being stopped from taking a bearing.

Comment/explanation

If the reasons for this CO's actions have not become apparent yet, perhaps I may enlighten the reader. It appears that his main concern was merely keeping himself out of trouble. This is not as difficult as it may appear because, by simply going through the motions, he avoided any direct involvement, and by tailoring the KTB entries to fit his motions, he deceived HQ at the same time.

The bearing obtained at some time between 0100 and 0130, for example, should have been transmitted at once, including the aircraft data. That means that U-764 would have been the first boat to do so and it is quite possible that we may have been ordered to act as shadower and transmit D/F-signals ourselves. The CO, however, had no intention of being involved in this manner, therefore, he waited until two other boats had transmitted their bearings before ordering transmission of ours. To conceal this delay and make it appear as if this bearing was up to date, he stated "Aircraft transmits D/F-signals" at 0200, thereby neatly linking the entry with the B-bar at 0220.

His failure of ordering observation of and bearings to be taken on the R/T-traffic rests upon the very same considerations; he wanted to avoid any close involvement, whenever possible. This was easy enough to achieve by simply ignoring the possibilities that R/T-bearings would have offered. However, there is no real point in going any further into this situation, except to say that if the R/T -traffic had been monitored continuously, the bearings thus obtained would have revealed that ONS-29 had passed the patrol lines probably by 2000 of the eighteenth (if not earlier) and the whole operation against this convoy could, and should, have been discontinued at that time.

The order of HQ (W/T 0326 of the nineteenth) that Vogler, Blauert, Bremen, and Dieterichs were to operate upon that convoy could not have been carried out anyway, because OL Blauert (U-734) was not even part of the patrol line due to being sunk on 9 February. KL Dieterichs (U-406) was out of action as well, having been sent to the bottom by HMS *Spey* in the early afternoon of the previous day. That left KL Vogler (U-212) and OL Bremen (U-764), but even if running at top speed and steering a course of about 165° - 170° true, in order to intercept ON-224 somewhere in square BE 42, neither boat could have reached that position by dawn because the distance was approximately 125-140 miles.

This, then, was the convoy battle that never was, resulting in the loss of three aircraft and three U-boats on our side, and HMS *Woodpecker* from the opposing forces.

HQ formally disbanded *Group Hai* by W/T 1255 of the nineteenth and transmitted a *post mortem* some thirteen hours later, stating that this operation had been undertaken by utilizing whatever forces were available at that time, in particular those of Air Group Atlantic. No success had been achieved as, due to engine problems, no reconnaissance missions could be flown during the crucial time on the eighteenth. Thus, the patrol lines could not be shifted to the best advantage during the last night, and there was no way this operation could have been continued during the day, as the few boats close to the convoy could not possibly have fought the carrier-borne planes which provided the convoy's air cover. A further such attack was to be made as soon as more boats could be led to a convoy and when the 37 mm AA-gun had become a more reliable weapon.

As we now know, no further such attempt was ever made. The time of the *old style* convoy battles and *wolf packs* was well and truly over. Any convoy under threat would be rerouted to avoid any patrol lines, or, it would be given reinforced defences by way of support groups with the sole task of hunting and sinking any *wolves* that may be bold enough to even approach a convoy.

Turning to the KTB entries, we find the W/T of this *post mortem* had not been entered, which may be considered as of no great importance. There are, however, other W/Ts that were of the utmost importance, yet they had also been omitted. The CO's deliberate disobedience of Serial Order No. 48/War Order 211a, in connection with the B-bar at 0220 on the nineteenth, has already been mentioned. What has not been illustrated is the cover he provided himself with in case his disobedience should become the subject of question.

That is to say, the W/Ts 1104 and 1137 of 22 January, containing the order for the alteration of the mentioned War Order, have not been entered in the KTB either. Nor, for that matter, did he enter W/T 0238 of 19 February, which admonished all boats to report bearings taken on aircraft beacon signals in accordance with the alteration of War Order 211a, namely by adding the aircraft's data (bearing on and distance from the convoy) to their own B-bar.

These omissions would give him a good excuse of being ignorant of those orders by pretending that they had not been received, thus neatly shifting the responsibility on to the shoulders of the communications department. We shall encounter other similar tactics presently and in the future. In contrast, it is quite remarkable to see how promptly this CO obeyed orders from HQ whenever it suited him to do so. For example, the entry at 0220 states that he was operating upon D/F-signals. However, the W/T 0208, entered at 0245, ordered the northern sectors of *Group Hai 1 & 2* to remain at the position reached, and the next entry reads: "Broke off operation." In other words, by obeying this order, he had been operating for a mere twenty-five minutes only

He then operates again as per the orders given in W/T 0326 (i.e. that Vogler, Blauert, Bremen, and Dieterichs are to operate upon the convoy at top speed) by steering 170° true, as he assumed the convoy to be on a heading of 225° true. As it happened, this course was approximately the correct one; however, his speed was incorrect. Covering some 40 miles in four hours can, by no stretch of the imagination, be called top speed. He then dived at daybreak (as ordered), still some 90 miles short of the convoy's position (ON-224), which could not have been reached even at top speed.

Other entries that the CO had made which are also false include the position of the convoy as per W/T 1633 of 17 February, which was entered as AL 8912. There is no such square, and the correct position (as in fact, given in the W/T) is AL 9812. Also, the serial number of W/T 2045 of the eighteenth, which was entered as 215 is also impossible on the Diana service, therefore, the correct one must be 715. However, there are further false entries that are far weightier than those quoted above.

As per KTB entries 13-3-44

The boat was in BF 4833 at 0000, surfaced at 0220 to charge its batteries, and had moved to BF 4679 by 0400.

At 0434, without having detected any prior radar search, an aircraft approached from 220° true, using its searchlight. In order to foil a bomb attack, the boat was turned away by applying hard rudder, but the aircraft attacked with gun-fire and dropped two magnesium flares. The gun-crews, manning the 20 mm twins, repulsed this attack immediately by well-placed anti-aircraft fire.

With W/T 0708, HQ reported an enemy aircraft to have been over a surfaced U-boat in BF 5174 at 0437, proceeding at 8 knots on a course of 90° true.

To this, the CO remarked: "that must have been the attacker."

The aircraft dropped a further magnesium flare in 80° true.

By B-bar 0443, the CO signaled the boat's arrival at the rendezvous with the escort in forty-eight hours, and he requested radio beacons for entering Brest.

Fifteen minutes later, he ordered B-bar 0458, reporting that the boat was being attacked by aircraft in BF 4687.

To this entry he added: "Radio room transmitted both signals in reverse order."

The boat dived two minutes after the last transmission and, proceeding at forty metres, was in BF 4982 at 0800 and in BF 4689 four hours later.

Facts

1) Transmission of anything at all is by order of the CO only. The entry "Radio room transmitted both signals in reverse order" is, therefore, false. The B-bar would have been transmitted as per his orders, and the onus is on him alone to give those orders clearly and correctly.

2) The B-bar "Being attacked by aircraft plus position and signature" was ciphered and ready for instant transmission before each surfacing of the boat, as are the other two B-bars mentioned previously in Chapter 2.

The aircraft attacked at 0434 (as per KTB) and the transmission of this signal should have been ordered at once. It was not.

Even if the two B-bar signals had been reversed, there was still a dangerous time-lag of some nine minutes. This was more than enough time to be damaged and rendered incapable of transmission, or even sunk.

3) Under entries at 0434, we find the W/T 0708 which could not have possibly been received some two and a half hours before transmission, which was at 0434. Furthermore, we dived at 0500 and unless the CO had ordered the boat to 16-18 metres for reception on VLF during the day (of which there is no evidence), this W/T could not have been received until surfacing again at 2150, approximately eighteen hours after it had already been entered in the KTB.

4) Linking this W/T with the attack on U-764 reveals, once again, more of the incompetence of this man as CO.

As per the W/T 0708, the aircraft was over a surfaced U-boat in BF 5174 at 0437, to which the CO stated that this must have been the attacker.

The boat's position at 0400 was given as BF 4679 and the attack occurred in BF 4687 at 0458, as per the B-bar. How, then, could this aircraft in BF 5174 possibly have been the attacker, when the boat at that time was in BF 4679 or BF 4687, some 70 miles away?

5) He was in BF 4687 at 0458, but at 0800 he stated to be in BF 4982. How did he manage to travel some 40 miles in three hours submerged? And, he traveled a similar distance during the next four hours, because at 1200 he was in BF 4689.

Comment/explanation

The statement made by the CO, "Radio room transmitted both signals in reverse order" is intended to conceal his own incompetence by shifting the blame for his incorrectly given orders onto the shoulders of the communications department as a whole. Simultaneously, he makes the individual appear to be incompetent, which he also does on a number of other occasions.

His own incompetence is emphasized by the fact that both transmission and receipt of the signal requesting escort and radio beacons would have been reported to him. He was, therefore, well aware of which signal had been transmitted at 0434, and the B-bar reporting the attack by aircraft should have been transmitted immediately thereafter. He, however, delayed for another fifteen minutes before ordering transmission of this signal—which was pointless because by that time, the attack had been repulsed and the boat went below two minutes later.

Apart from attempting to conceal his own incompetence by making the personnel in the radio room appear to be at fault, the question is posed as to whether or not there was a different, underlying motive for his actions. I cannot say there was, however, one cannot exclude the possibility that there may have been, for he may have thought it expedient to guard against any undesirable leaks. That is to say, he was quite safe from any direct exposure on account of being forced to go through channels. A leak, however, could have presented him with some problems.

There was, for example, his refusal of permitting a bearing to be taken on the R/T-traffic of SC-152, and his subsequent order to falsify my radio report so as to conceal his own omission of these events from the KTB.

As indicated in the previous chapter, I had mentioned these points to the Flotilla Communications Officer when handing in my report, and there is a possibility, however remote it may appear, that such facts may leak through to the CO of the Flotilla (KK Lehmann-Willenbrock), resulting in questions being asked. However, as the flotilla is also supplied with a copy of the KTB, the CO's entry as to the "incompetence of the radio personnel" would have been sufficient to dismiss any such leak as undeserving of further inquiry.

The remaining facts do not really require further elucidation as they are self-explanatory, and the false KTB entries reveal his incompetence far better than anything else could.

We are now left to observe the summary made by the CO of this mission.

As per KTB entries 15-3-44

We are told that advantage had been taken of the experiences gained from the boat's first mission. Changing over from day to night routine proved beneficial, and the quality of the boat's atmosphere, while traveling submerged, was noticeably better as during the first mission.

Attacks by aircraft, with or without prior radar location, could be met by rapid changes in both course and speed. Success on the convoy did not materialize due to unfavourable visibility and a strong defence force.

Facts

By means of the last statement in this summary, the CO, again, delivers his own proof of his deceitfulness. Turning back to the relevant entries pertaining to convoy ON-222, we find:

3-2-44

2002 Medium swell from the west; Good visibility

4-2-44

0009 Medium swell from the west; Moonlight, Good visibility
0108 The convoy sometimes disappears in a cloud coming up from the west, or in the reflected light of the moon
0245 Medium visibility
0400 Unchanged (visibility)

There is no mention of unfavorable visibility in any of these entries.

During this time, he had every opportunity for achieving success by attacking the convoy, or the stern escorts, or both. The boat's presence had not been detected even after HMCS *Ottawa* had obtained a correct H/F D/F bearing on our transmission at 0009, though incorrectly estimating the distance to be more than 30 miles.

Comment/explanation

His statement is blatantly false because he had only himself to blame for any lack of success. The targets were presented before him under circumstances that could not have possibly been bettered. This statement, therefore, could have only been made to conceal his incompetence. In fact, OL Boddenberg attacked this very same convoy, though without achieving any success due to unexplained torpedo failures. However, there was no mention in his KTB of "unfavorable visibility" or a "strong defence force" stopping him from doing so.

Conclusion

It has been said that the personnel at HQ did not miss much; however, both in this instance and in many others (as will be seen in due course),

With music provided, U-764 entered the U-boat pen in Brest, 15 March 1944.

Inspection of the crew of U-764 by Commander Lehmann-Willenbrock, the Chief of the 9th U-boat flotilla, upon arrival of the boat in Brest on 15 March 1944.

"Umpah-pah" accompanied U-764 into the pen in Brest, 15 March 1944.

Some of the crew of U-764 on the quarter-deck upon arrival in Brest on 15 March 1944. The author is at the extreme left.

they have certainly been deceived. It is true, of course, that HQ had only the KTB upon which to base an opinion, but they have not been sufficiently alert to spot the falsities produced by this CO.

The planned *old style* convoy battle with ONS-29 never materialized, and no blame can be attached to this CO for that. However, he had every opportunity for action on ON-222—yet there was none. All we have are his KTB entries by means of which he would have us believe that he made every effort, but failed through no fault of his own.

How HQ had been fooled by this CO's KTB entries can be gauged by Rear-Admiral Godt's opinion, when he said that the boat, after all its efforts of reaching the front of the convoy, had been deprived of success by bad visibility at the decisive moment. "...[I]n spite of unfavorable circumstances, the CO, attack-spirited, tried to get into a firing position; success, alas, was denied him."

A week later, the question of making an effort with regard to SC-152 did not even arise. The CO simply denied the presence of this convoy, blocked the taking of a bearing on its R/T, omitted any reference to it in his KTB, and ensured that my radio report contained no mention of it either; lest the personnel at HQ question his actions.

After two months at sea, the only visible result of an effort made is his production of falsely documented events to cover his lamentable performance, as well as the return of 11 torpedoes, as good as new.

U-764 arriving in Brest, 15 March 1944

Chapter Five

Hush-Hush Into the Channel

Third Mission
18 to 28 May 1944

In contrast to the longest mission, there now follows the shortest. The boat had been fitted with a schnorkel and, together with some other boats (U-269, U-441, U-953, and U-984), had been sent on a very special mission into the British West-Channel. The forthcoming operation was shrouded in great secrecy, and initially only the Flotilla Chief, his Executive Officer, the Communications Officer, and the boat's CO had knowledge of the destination.

As for the crew, this was staged to be an "alarm exercise," and the boat was moved out of the pen into the roadstead, where fresh provisions were delivered by lighter and KK Lehmann-Willenbrock, the CO of the flotilla, came on board to reveal the true nature of this exercise.

Whether all this secrecy was of any practical value must be seriously questioned. After all, the boat was now in the roadstead in full view of anybody who cared to look. The Flotilla Chief could be seen coming on board and addressing the mustered crew on the quarterdeck, fresh provisions were taken on, and the boat cleared the harbour while there was still daylight. Under these circumstances, its departure could not possibly have been concealed, and the whole exercise appeared to be rather pointless.

The objective of this mission was, in the first instance, to ascertain whether the schnorkel would permit the boats to operate in shallow waters on the enemy's doorstep without being located. And secondly, to gather information with regard to the enemy's air surveillance as well as guarding against a possible surprise landing or invasion attempt by giving warning of such moves.

We were sent hither and thither without making direct contact with surface vessels of any kind. On 23 May, however, we received orders to surface, and were promptly attacked by aircraft.

As per KTB entries 23-5-44

These boats had been designated *Group Dragoner,* and at 0000, U-764 was in BF 2921 charging its batteries by means of schnorkel.

Some two hours later, the W/T 0049, addressed to *Group Dragoner,* had been received from Captain U-boats West, and both U-764 and U-441 were ordered to surface because the enemy had been located in BF 2921, the very square that this boat was in!

Schnorkelling finished at 0225. whereupon weak hydrophone bearings had been picked up in 117° true, which did coincide with the direction of the enemy location as given by the W/T. The boat surfaced ten minutes later in a smooth sea, steering 117° true and detected radar search in both 0° and 180° true. In order to take the radar location bow-on, thus presenting the smallest silhouette, the boat was then turned onto 180° true, yet twenty minutes later, a third radar source was coming in from 90° true, its volume increasing.

Barely five minutes had elapsed, when the boat, at 0250 and in BF 2679, was attacked by gun-fire from a twin-engined aircraft, causing slight injury to one of the AA-gunners. While the radar pulses continued, the boat was attacked again from the air, but without suffering any damage.

The third attack followed at 0301. Six bombs were dropped this time, but those disappeared harmlessly into the sea astern on the boat's starboard side. There was no damage by gun-fire, and the boat remained clear to dive.

By B-bar signal at 0304, the CO reported to have been spotted by aircraft and then ordered the boat below. While diving, sea water penetrated through the round dipol's cable duct on the bridge into the sound room, where the previously obtained hydrophone bearing was found to be slowly disappearing in 100° true. The boat then moved off in the direction of 270° and was, at 0400, in BF 2913.

Facts

The B-bar at 0304 on the twenty-third was quite inappropriate. Having been attacked by aircraft three times within the preceding fifteen minutes, the signal should have stated "Being attacked by aircraft" plus the boat's position, rather than "Aircraft have been spotted," and no position at all. Furthermore, the CO was wasting valuable time here by having this signal enciphered, whereas the correct one was ready for instant transmission as per the standing orders previously indicated in Chapter 2.

The entry at 0301, stating "No damage by gun-fire," is also false. Though the boat itself may have suffered no damage as such, one of the attacker's bullets did penetrate the tube which housed the cable of the round-dipol on the bridge.

We went below four minutes later, sea water entered through the holed tube, issued at the cable's exit in the sound room and drenched the 40-watt short wave transmitter beneath. The cable had to be cut in order to seal the duct, and the aerial for radar detection was, therefore, out of action.

Upon return to base, the transmitter had to be taken off, dried out, tested, and repaired as necessary. The holed tube on the bridge had to be replaced and a new cable threaded through and fitted. Although all this may appear to be of little importance, it is, nevertheless, "damage by gun-fire."

Comment/explanation

Here again, this CO revealed both his gross incompetence and his arrogant insubordination.

The two B-bar signals "Being attacked by aircraft" and "Being attacked by destroyer," plus the boat's position in each case, had been ordered to be enciphered and ready for instant transmission before each surfacing. The reason for this is to give HQ at least a clue as to where and by what means a boat had been lost, and in case of damage to the boat and abandonment by the crew, where a possible rescue mission might be undertaken by another boat in the vicinity.

It is, therefore, vital to transmit the correct signal and to do so at once, during the very first attack. His initial hesitation of fifteen minutes before ordering the transmission of a signal could have been detrimental to both the boat and the crew, not to mention the fact that the signal which was ordered to be transmitted, after the third attack, was inaccurate. Had those six bombs sunk the boat, HQ would have been totally in the dark regarding its loss, nor could a rescue mission have been even attempted in case of damage or to pick up the crew. All this rested on the shoulders of the CO to take the appropriate action, which, in this case, he did not do. Ultimately, there is no justification for his putting the boat and its crew in jeopardy.

Two boats of *Group Dragoner*, Bremen and Hartmann, were then ordered to dive (which the former had done already), and Bremen was told to commence return journey.

Before closing this chapter, we should look at one or two other points.

As per KTB entries 22-5-44

The Etmal at 1200 was given as "surfaced" = 31.6 sm.

24-5-44

Again, the Etmal was given as "surfaced" = 20.2 sm.

28-5-44

Upon arrival in Brest, at 0500, the Etmal is stated to have been 21.9 sm on the surface, 14.5 sm submerged, making a total of 35.5.

Facts

The entries of 22 & 24 May are false, for at no point during the preceding 24-hour period had the boat been on the surface. The total of the entry for 28 May is false as well, as is obvious.

Comment/explanation

Incompetent log-keeping, as before, and his arithmetic had not improved any either.

As per KTB entries 23-5-44

At 0000, the boat was submerged in BF 2921. At 0236, we surfaced and traveled initially on a course of 117° true and changed to 180° true shortly thereafter.

The boat was on the surface in BF 2679 at 0250 (where the three attacks by aircraft occurred), dived at 0305, moved off in the direction of 270° true, and was in BF 2913 at 0400.

U-764's route, 19-28 May 1944. On 23 May, at 0000, the boat was in BF 2921.

The KTB then states these courses:

0225 = 117°
0236 = 180°
0305 = 270°
0315 = 0°

How could he have reached BF 2679, at 0400, on those headings?

On 26 May, he was in BF 5212 for 12 hours. He then turned away to the southwest and went to BF 5138, before again turning in the direction of Brest. Why this diversion?

51°N
50°N
49°N
48°N
8°W
7°W
6°W
5°W
4°W
3°W
2°W
1°W
0°W
13
21
16
24
25
26
19
27
28
43
51
52
31
32
Lands End
Lizard Hd.
Brest
26 May
27 May
04 00
00 00
23 May

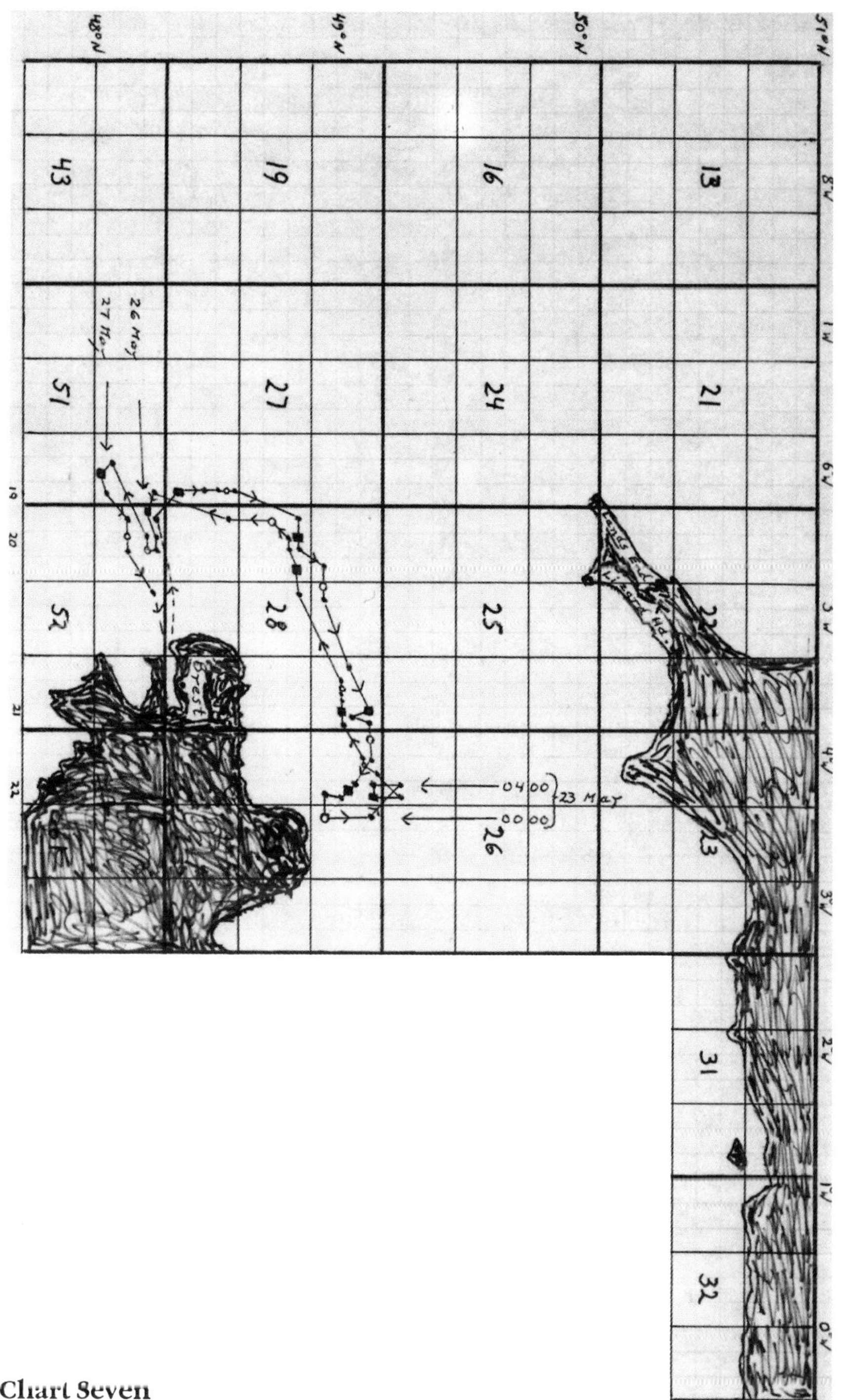

Chart Seven

Facts

It is quite impossible to go from BF 2921 to BF 2679 on either a course of 117° or one of 180°. The correct course would have to have been about 320° true. Likewise, fifteen minutes later, at 0250, he moved off from BF 2679 in direction of 270°, and an hour's travel on this heading brought him to BF 2913 at 0400—at least according to his KTB. However, to go from BF 2679 to BF 2913 can only be done by steering 180° true (Compare Chart 7).

Comment/explanation

This does not really require any further explanation, for the facts reveal his incompetence far better than anything else could.

Conclusion

Whether the mission be one of two months duration or lasts a mere ten days, the length of time does not make the slightest difference; the recurrence of the incompetence of this CO is present regardless.

A signal, stating "Being attacked by aircraft" plus the boat's position, surely includes the fact that we had been spotted. The contents of the signal ordered was, therefore, not only wrong (it gave no position) and inappropriate (it gave no indication of an attack), but it also revealed his total disregard of the standing orders.

Whether it had been in response to these events or not, I cannot say, however, perhaps it should be mentioned at this point that a change in the procedure had been ordered less than three weeks later regarding the transmission of the B-Bar "Being attacked by aircraft, square...."

On 9 June, a correction to Serial Order 39 had been transmitted on all services, stating that when a U-boat is attacked by aircraft, the W/T operator should transmit the respective signal on his own initiative immediately on receiving the order "Aircraft."

Although this may appear to be an improvement, unfortunately, it did not go far enough. If the single word "Aircraft," uttered on the bridge, is merely taken as referring to the attacker and does not reach the radio room at all, it could have left the boat in a worse position than before. A far better solution to this problem would have been to give the W/T-operator authority to transmit the said B-bar immediately when he became aware of the boat's AA-guns firing. The only exception would be practice firing, which should be announced as such well in advance.

Chapter Six

Into the Fray On D-Day

Fourth Mission
6 to 23 June 1944

Following this brief test mission, U-764 had been restocked (except for fresh provisions) and placed on six-hourly standby for the expected invasion from the other side of the Channel.

Although it had been fully recognized that only boats equipped with a schnorkel could operate in certain areas, when the fateful day dawned, all boats ready to sail, whether with or without schnorkel, were sent to the Channel with orders to attack the invasion fleet regardless of their own safety. These orders were amplified in a number of W/Ts, one of which bears the time 2301 on 6 June, was in Officer's Cypher, and had been addressed to Channel boats only. It states that the decisive hour of the war was upon us, and therefore, the admiral of the fleet had ordered this group of boats to operate in the Channel because the situation demanded that every action was to be taken.

Other W/Ts (2319 of 6 June and 0025 and 0111 of 7 June), addressed to all Commanding Officers at sea, stated that

> at this time, more than any other time before, the future of the German people depends also upon the U-boat arm. BdU, therefore, demands all-out operation, even if the consequence should be the loss of one's own boat. Any thought of precautionary measures are to be put aside, instead, every vessel concerned in the landing is to be attacked regardless of what may follow, for every man and every weapon destroyed before reaching the beaches will decrease the enemy's prospects of success. BdU relies on his

U-boatmen to carry out the orders given.

A further W/T (2329 of 11 June) said much the same, including that

> the invasion fleet is to be attacked with complete recklessness, because every vessel, even if it puts no more than fifty men or one tank ashore, must be a U-boat's target, calling for all-out effort. No heed is to be paid to any danger while operating in shallow waters or in the vicinity of possible mine-fields; the enemy is to be attacked at all costs. A U-boat, which inflicts losses on the enemy during the landing operations, has discharged its highest duty and has justified its existence, even if it does not survive.

In fact, only very few did survive, for the boats had been set upon a hopeless task. There have even been rumours (after the War) to the effect that "Kamikaze-Orders" had been issued. That is to say, any boat, having expended all torpedoes, was supposed to ram anything within their reach; but no substantiation for such rumours could be found.

Following the orders of the C-in-C, a total of thirty-five boats sailed from France on D-day: fifteen from Brest, fourteen from St. Nasaire, four from La Pallice, and two from Lorient. The boats without schnorkel did not stand a chance; all were either sunk or severely damaged by aircraft. This resulted in the order of 10 June that no more non-schnorkel boats were to be sent into the Channel.

That left the schnorkel boats on their own. Although they did go into the Channel and operate, they were few in number and their chances of survival were not much better. Of seven schnorkel boats from Brest, for example, (U-269, Uhl; U-441, KL Hartmann; U-621, OL Stuckmann U-984, OL Sieder; U-275, OL Bork; U-764, OL Bremen; and U-953, OL Marbach) the first four were sunk between 18 June and 20 August, U-275 was mined in March 1945 and only the last two survived to the end of hostilities.

U-764 sailed at 1450 on 6 June, and as the CO had not sunk anything yet (though he did claim having sunk a destroyer during the first mission), nor had he fired a single torpedo since the end of November 1943, his track-record can only be described as extremely poor. At this point, however, he intended to change all that by having a shooting spree, thereby revealing his "attack-spirited" nature.

As per KTB entries 8/9-6-44

The boat was in BF 2852 at 2000, and slightly more than an hour later, the W/T 1730 advised that, during the night of 8/9 June, four destroyers would be making a high-speed run from Brest to Cherbourg.

At 0150 of the ninth, the boat was said to be in the same square and the previously mentioned popping and whizzing noises had ceased, but diesel after diesel were overrunning the boat from east to west.

Observations by periscope revealed star-shells and marker-flares, and it was assumed that our own destroyers had probably encountered an enemy convoy.

Overrunning of the boat continued, and the CO did not dare surface for fear of being run over; he presumed that this was an armada of landing vessels. His intention was to go to twenty metres and fire by hydrophone bearings.

At 0245, in BF 2853, he fired a T5 from Tube I toward a particularly strong bearing in 90° true, followed by another T5 from the stern tube toward an equally strong bearing in 170° true. The first detonation occurred after fifteen minutes, twenty-five seconds, followed by the second two minutes later.

The running of the torpedoes could be monitored by hydrophone for a short time only, as they were being drowned out by propeller noises, but the last detonation was followed by several others.

At 0322, in BF 3856, propeller noises (diesel) were moving from west to east. He fired two FATs from Tubes II & III toward a strong noiseband in 70° true. Firing angle had been set at 50° with a long left loop at 3,000 and 4,000 metres.

Nine and a half minutes after firing, two harsh torpedo detonations had been heard, but these were assumed to have occurred at the end of their run.

He fired another T5 from Tube IV toward strong propeller noises in 80° true, at 0342. This torpedo jammed in the tube, running there for twenty-seven seconds. No observations had been made within the boat.

Three minutes later, U-764 retired for reloading on a course of 330° true, and the propeller noises slowly disappeared in the east.

The boat was in BF 2856 at 0400, and the CO stated that according to both W/Ts and the German Forces report there had been a destroyer battle at the west exit of the Channel. He described it as peculiar that all propeller noises had been classified "diesel" and that at least thirty had been involved.

Facts

Here we had an "attack-spirited" CO, firing five torpedoes (one being a non-runner) within an hour by hydrophone bearings—and hitting nothing!

In this instance, it was all to the good because he had totally ignored the warning given by W/T 1730 on the eighth, and received almost six hours prior to shooting, regarding the four German destroyers passing

U-764's route, as per KTB, 6-22 June 1944.

9 June, at 0245 in BF 2853
at 0322 in BF 3856
at 0400 in BF 2856

This represents a distance of 220 miles in 1-1/4 hours. The lack of precision in his log-keeping is quite obvious.

HMS *Blackwood* torpedoed at 1907 on 15 June in BF 3513.

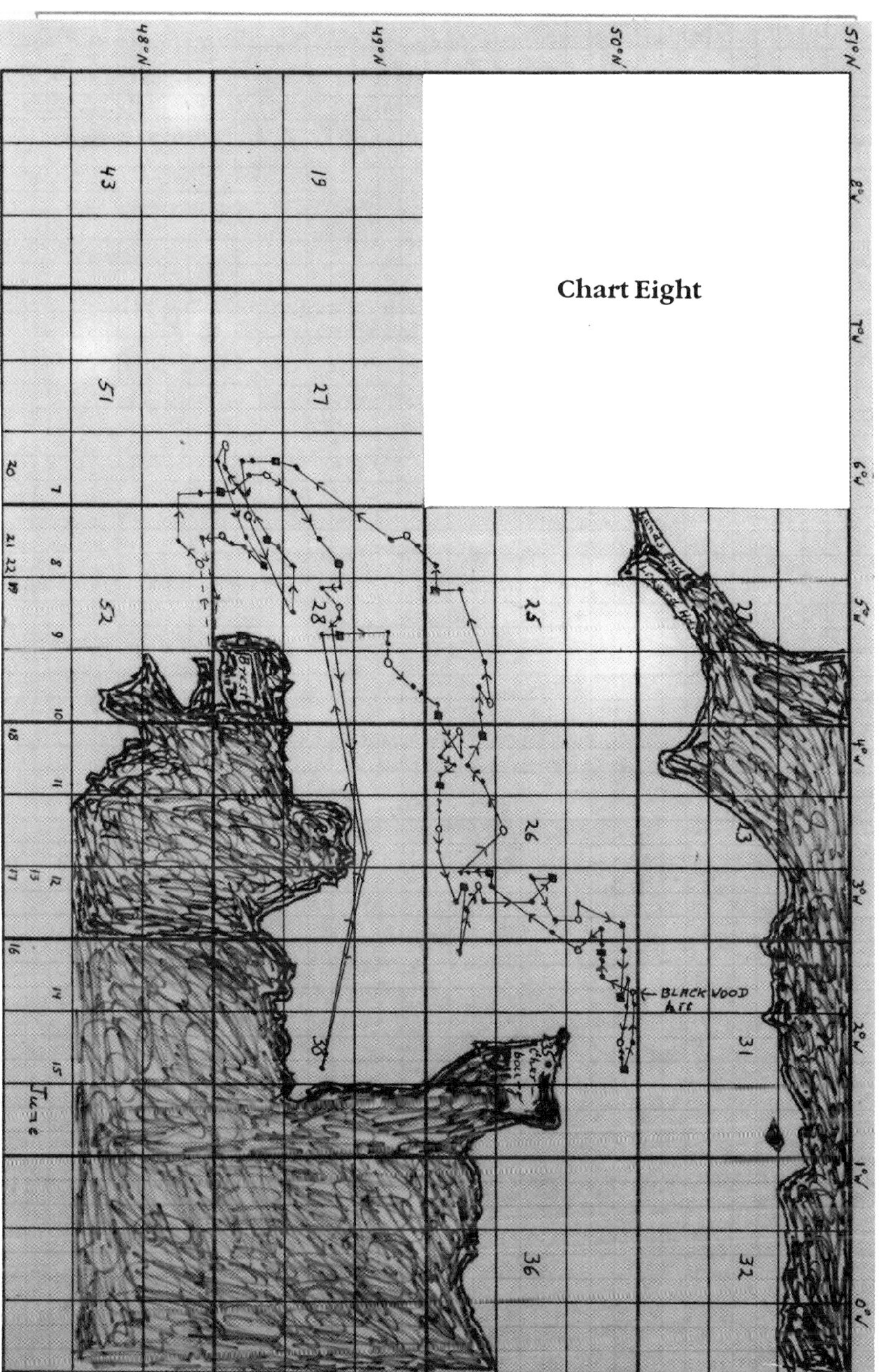

Chart Eight

through the area. He then concealed both his gross stupidity and his arrogant disregard of the warning given by the entry of 0400. Besides, the position entered at 0322 is far removed from the west exit of the Channel and will hardly permit the boat to float, let alone make a submerged attack, for he is almost on dry land! (see Chart 8.)

Comment/explanation

Apart from hydrophone bearings, the man had no data whatsoever; there was no reading available for distance, course, speed, angle, or inclination. He also did not know whether the targets were friend or foe. Whether or not there was a destroyer battle in progress is quite irrelevant because it was not necessary to intervene in the circumstances stated. There was no evidence of any W/T or the Forces Report mentioning a destroyer battle at the time of his shooting spree.

His false entries are merely another attempt at concealing his gross incompetence, thereby hoping to escape the consequences. This attempt was in vain, for it actually highlighted his failings, however, his arrogance blinds him even to that fact.

The Chief of Operations, however, was not so blinded, as is evident by his opinion to this KTB, when he stated:

> This mission into the Channel was unsatisfactory. The task was attacking the invasion traffic between the English south coast and the Seine-basin, regardless of the consequences. This task had been approached without energy and the will to attack, which was demanded in this of all situations.
>
> ...The firing of four torpedoes on 9 June was a total waste, because no data of any kind had been obtained by periscope observations and even the distance to the targets could not be ascertained by hydrophone alone. It is quite wrong to use the sound bearing for a random shot without even identifying the target.
>
> ...It had been made known that four German destroyers would be on passage from Brest to Cherbourg which, as subsequently established, had been in the firing range of this particular boat at the time in question.

This kind of shooting could have been employed to his advantage on convoy ON-222, on 3/4 February (Chapter 2), but on that occasion he did not act. Indeed, the Chief of Operations stated on that occasion that there had been opportunity to shoot sightless by sound bearings from a depth of sixty metres while the boat was being overrun by the convoy.

As per KTB entries 15-6-44

The boat was in BF 3522 at 0000, and an hour later, during an all-round search by periscope, the CO observed red-light from an aircraft on two occasions.

There were no hydrophone bearings at that time.

At 0130, we are told that continuous patrol activities were making it difficult to recharge the batteries during schnorkelling and that he had reversed course, steering 270° true, in order to go to Peter Port to recharge there. To this he added "The crew is badly in need of a day's rest."

0400 found the boat in BF 3522. Schnorkelling had ceased at 0444, and at 0600, still in the same position, a flotilla of minesweepers passed in front of the boat on a northerly course.

At 0800, U-764 had moved one square to the east, to BF 3523, but four hours thereafter was said to be in BF 3521, and the etmal on submerged travel was given as 40 miles.

A fast escort vessel passed at 1400 on a northerly course, at a distance of 4,000 metres and two hours later, the boat had shifted position by one square to the west, to BF 3513.

At 1900, still in the same square, one fast escort vessel and one frigate were passing behind the boat to the south. At a distance of about 1,000 metres on the boat's port beam, the escort vessel changed course by 90° and ran into the CO's sights in 330° true.

Seven minutes on, he fired a spread of two torpedoes from tubes I & IV, resulting in a loud detonation after one minute, thirty-four seconds. The target is said to be enveloped in a large brown cloud, and after this had cleared, the vessel, type "Atherstone," was seen to be lying dead in the water. The whole fore-ship had been torn away up to the bridge and the mast was bent.

The vessel's stern had risen, and the frigate hesitatingly approached the target area, while a second vessel came into view form 300° true.

At 1930, U-764 was on a course of 180° true, when the frigate suddenly increased speed, rounded the stricken escort and headed toward the suspected attacker's position. The CO then stated that the boat did not turn fast enough for a T5 shot from the stern tube.

While going down to fifty metres, the frigate sped past the boat's stern, but doubt was expressed as to whether she had seen the boat. But three minutes later, the boat was shaken by two violent explosions, which were assumed to have been scare bombs launched by thrower.

The resulting damage was listed as follows: No view to be had through the periscope, the torpedo in the stern tube was jammed, the cooling water conduit of the electric motors had been torn twice, the aft hydroplanes were very noisy, as was the starboard shaft, ballast tank number 1 was torn and the water-tight stern could not be closed. There was also breakage of glass and a number of fuses were blown.

The boat was still in the same square at 2000, while both the frigate and the other vessel were aimlessly chasing about on top.

One series of D/Cs had been dropped seven minutes later, but no further damage was caused thereby. The boat, running silently, then moved off to the south on a course of 250° true. Extensive search activities still continued on the surface, whereas the onsetting ebb-tide helped the boat to drift away from the firing position quickly.

Conditions for sound detection were, fortunately, very bad, and all unnecessary equipment had been switched off. The boat was on a westerly heading, proceeding at a slow speed on one electric motor, and doubt was expressed as to the possibility of recharging batteries during the coming night.

Facts

The vessel torpedoed was HMS *Blackwood,* and when the two fish left their tubes, the top of the conning tower briefly broke surface. There is no mention of this occurrence in the KTB, except in an oblique way by the statement "Whether she (the frigate) has seen the boat is doubtful."

As luck would have it, we had, apparently not been spotted, but the frigate (HMS *Duckworth*) certainly did not throw mere "scare bombs" as stated in the KTB. She obviously came in for the kill.

The CO of HMS *Duckworth* reported (ADM 199/472) that at 1910, HMS *Blackwood*, in company with HMS *Essington* three miles on her starboard quarter, was traveling at 16 knots on a course of about 300° true, in order to form a line abreast and "Gamma search" together with HMS *Duckworth*.

A minute later, while this formation was proceeding at 12 knots on a heading of 335° true, HMS *Blackwood* erupted in a violent explosion and became enveloped in a dense cloud of yellow smoke which obscured the vessel. After this had cleared, HMS *Duckworth*, three miles on HMS *Blackwood's* port beam, observed the latter minus her fore-ship, which had been blown away. Her mast had collapsed and the bridge structure had been flattened aback. HMS *Duckworth* with HMS *Dommett* then closed from the west, whereas HMS *Essington* was ordered to stand by the wreck.

It was assumed that HMS *Blackwood* had been torpedoed from her starboard side, and it was considered probable that the U-boat would seek to escape on a southeasterly course, or go to the bottom.

At 1927, HMS *Duckworth*, while passing astern of the wreck, obtained an asdic contact at 1,300 yards on a bearing of 70°. The target, slowly moving to the right, was estimated to be traveling at 2 knots on a course of 130° true, and HMS *Duckworth*, proceeding at 8 knots, attacked with hedgehogs. Explosions occurred simultaneously six seconds after the

HMS Wildgoose *photographed from the aircraft carrier HMS* Tracker, *date and location unknown.*

HM ships Berry, Duckworth, *and* Essington, *date and location unknown (courtesy of IWM)*

HM ships Wildgoose *and* Starling *in Liverpool, February 1944. (courtesy of IWM)*

HMCS Dunver, *date and location unknown (courtesy of National Maritime Museum)*

projectiles struck the water.

Although a stream of oil bubbles rose to the surface, it could not be established whether they emanated from a U-boat or might have come from a wreck, and all contact was suddenly lost.

As there was no conclusive evidence of the U-boat having been destroyed, the search continued with HMS *Duckworth*, HMS *Dommett*, and HMS *Essington*. The group was subsequently reinforced by HMS *Starling* and HMS *Wildgoose*, plus HMS *Braithwaite* joining the search the following morning; but no sign of the U-boat could be found.

The conclusion was that the HMS *Blackwood* had been hit in her forward magazine by a torpedo fired from her starboard side, and in the absence of any definite proof, it was suggested that the attacking U-boat may have been destroyed by HMS *Duckworth*. The survivors of HMS *Blackwood* had all been evacuated by air-sea rescue launches and were taken to Portland.

For once, the KTB entries of the actual attack are in accord with the facts, but this CO's incompetence is, nevertheless, plainly evident with regard to the subsequent events. He first stated "the frigate hesitatingly approached the target area" and then "the boat did not turn fast enough for a T5 shot form the stern tube." He had been aware of the frigate's presence from the start and he should have anticipated a counter-attack by her in any event. Therefore, instead of merely sitting at the periscope and observing the effects of his hit on HMS *Blackwood*, he should have at least tried turning the boat right away, thus he might have had a chance of a shot at her when she advanced toward the area, thereby possibly preventing her counter-attack altogether.

The boat's stern had been severely damaged by at least one of the hedgehogs fired by HMS *Duckworth*, and it was only pure luck and thanks to the bad asdic conditions that the hunters lost contact and U-764 got away.

Another statement displaying the CO's incompetence is the one made at 1933: "Two violent explosions shake the boat. Probably scare bombs launched by thrower."

It is difficult to imagine that a man of this status could believe that these U-boat hunters would be content with merely scaring off their quarry; particularly since there were four of them on anti-submarine patrol, and one of their own had just been torpedoed. Hunting teams, such as this one, were not known for simply scaring their adversaries. It is clear that their intentions were to destroy, which is apparent form the damage that was listed in the KTB and what was seen in dry dock.

The Chief of Operations continued his comment on this unsatisfactory mission by stating:

> In spite of the strictest orders, notwithstanding the good chances of

reaching the operational area north of the Seine-bay, the task has been abandoned prematurely without sufficient reason for so doing. Following a comparatively trouble-free approach, the boat had advanced to the area below Cherbourg. Then, however, without being particularly pressured by the enemy, the CO decided on going on to Peter Port to recharge the batteries, and to give the crew a rest.

This decision was wrong, for on the one hand, he had managed to recharge batteries a sea previously without encountering any difficulties, and on the other, the favourable position short of the operational area had to be held. The latter applies even further because the conditions within the enemy's stream of traffic would presumably be less strenuous, due to the pell-mell of vessels, than the way through the heavily patrolled approach area.

Having missed his big chance, the CO was promptly punished by a D/C-pursuit, which finally forced him to turn for base.

Although this CO would not hesitate in making false KTB entries when there is an opportunity for vilifying the personnel of the communications department, he did omit entering the boat breaking surface, for this was, of course, the LI's fault. It would not have been in his best interest to expose a fellow officer's shortcomings–in particular under the circumstances prevailing at that time–as this could easily backfire on him by leading to the exposure of his own incompetence.

In addition, there are the following entries: on the ninth, at 0245, he was in BF 2853; at 0322 in BF 3856; and at 0400 in BF 2856. The entry at 0322 is, therefore, patently false. (see Chart 8)

If anyone be tempted to now say that this should read BF 2856, then my reply is that we are not in the least concerned with what an entry *should* have been, but what it *actually* was. One must remember that the CO is responsible for ensuring that his KTB is correct before putting his name on it and have it sent to eight recipients.

On the same day, the ninth, the serial number of W/T 1322 was entered as 815. This is also false because the preceding W/T 1158 bears the number 816 and the following W/T 1350 carries 818. The correct number, therefore, must be 817.

From 2000 on the fourteenth to 0600 on the fifteenth, he was in BF 3522. Yet, as per the KTB, he was schnorkelling and, since 0130, was steering a course of 270° true. It is impossible to comprehend this idle behavior of ten hours.

What is stranger still is the position given two hours later, at 0800, of BF 3523. This implies that six and one-half hours on a heading of 270° true would take the boat to a position east of that which was held previously.

On the fifteenth, at 2017, the CO stated: "Moved off to the south...course = 250° true."

Apart from missing his tactical classes, he must have been absent during navigational lessons as well because a course of 250° true would not take the boat anywhere near a southern direction.

On the sixteenth, the etmal is given as 45.6 sm on the surface, whereas the boat had not surfaced even once during this mission.

There is also the entry of 0130 on 15 June which states: "Reversed course in order to recharge batteries in Peter Port. The crew is badly in need of a day's rest." Apart from the CO having little or no regard for the crew anyway, we had been at sea, at this stage, for less than nine days. Why then did he display this sudden concern for the welfare of the crew?

In order to understand this puzzle, one must return to 9 June. On that day, the W/T 1350 ordered four boats, including U-764, to concentrate their main effort in BF 3610. However, he never took the boat to that position. He, as we have seen, remained for ten hours in BF 3522, briefly grazing BF 3523, and then went westward on the pretext of looking after the crew.

There is one final point to be made. In his own summary, the CO stated that minesweeping activities during daylight had been observed in the direction from east to west and also on a line form BF 3511 to BF 3561. It is impossible to visualize how he observed activities alleged to stretch into BF 3561 when he was never even anywhere near that position, as Chart 8 clearly illustrates. Those activities may have been detected in BF 3511, but there is no way of determining the line of such sweep once the vessels concerned had disappeared from sight.

Conclusion

During this mission, he fired seven torpedoes in all. The first five (one being a non-runner) went against indefinite targets. Obviously, he did not know what he was firing at, nor did he have the appropriate data for his shots. It was fortunate that he obtained no hits, for if he had, the victims of his stupidity would most likely have been our own destroyers.

Following this fiasco, he pretended to follow orders, but he never went as far as the operational area assigned. Instead, he took recourse to a more favourable position, in his opinion, in order to keep himself out of trouble. He reversed course, and ultimately brought on trouble to himself by confronting a team of four U-boat hunters.

True, he may have had sight of only two of them at that stage, but he fired two fish at HMS *Blackwood*, obtained one hit, and risked the loss of boat and crew because he did not turn the boat and stop HMS *Duckworth* in her tracks, with the intentions of preventing the counter-attack by her.

The damage suffered by this counter-attack fortunately did not sink the

Eight of U-764's thirteen Petty Officers in Brest, June 1944. Back row from left: Gerhard Siegel - CPO, Heinz Guske - PO Telegraphist, Jochen Kaiser - PO Control Room, and unidentified - PO Diesel Engines. Front row from left: Karl Müller - PO Electric Motors, unidentified - PO Torpedo Mechanic, "Jupp" (Joseph ?) - Bootsmaat, and Werner Schulz - PO Telegraphist.

The author in Brest, July 1944

boat, but it had been sufficient to force termination of the mission. Only pure luck and bad asdic conditions enabled us to get away and reach Brest.

The depth of this man's incompetence is nearly unbelievable.

One of the 5-kilowatt transmitters used by the radio room of U-boat HQ some 25-30 miles away, spring 1942. On the left is a 150-watt long wave transmitter as used on a U-boat.

Chapter Seven

Repeat Performance

Fifth Mission
6 August to 19 September 1944

As a result of the CO's incompetence, the dockyards had been given work to do, and the damage sustained during the previous mission kept the boat out of commission for the next six weeks. In the meantime, the invasion had progressed, and it had become quite obvious that Brest would be falling into enemy hands sooner or later and we would, therefore, not be returning there.

On 6 August, at 2215, U-764 quietly sneaked out of the pen and sailed for the Channel again. Right from the start, extensive activities by both single patrol vessels and U-boat hunting groups had been encountered, but the CO had still not caught on to the fact that the Kreissaege (circular saw) was not a U-boat detection device but a noise buoy (CAT) towed behind patrolling, escorting, and hunting vessels in order to attract acoustic torpedoes, thus protecting the vessel itself from being hit.

Streamed CATs did, in fact, provide a measure of protection for us as well. On the one hand, their noise could be heard from a distance greater than that of the towing vessel's engines or propellers. On the other hand, a CAT's noise easily drowned out any noise made by a U-boat, thereby precluding the detection of the latter by the enemy's sound search.

The mentioned anticipation of not returning to Brest was proven correct shortly thereafter, as shown by the W/T 2107 of 15 August, which ordered the Channel boats to proceed to Norway after conclusion of their mission. They were further ordered to report their position by short-signal (B-bar) after passing the longitude of square BE 23, thereby indicating that passage to Norway had been commenced. Only boats unable to reach Norway, due to insufficient fuel, were to go to Bordeaux.

The mission of U-764 had not yet reached that stage, and for the time being, the CO had some more shooting to do.

As per KTB entries 17-8-44

At 0930, in BF 3197, a hospital-ship passed on a course to the south.

In the same square, at 1300, a wide sound-band moved through the area from north to south. Through sheets of rain, the shadows of steamers appeared now and again at a distance of 80 hectometres.

At 1347, he fired a T5-shot from the stern tube at a laden freighter of 5,000 GRT on positive data. Though the torpedo could still be heard running near the target twelve minutes later, the steamer, laterally separated from the convoy, sailed on. The CO presumed there had been a malfunction of the firing pistol.

At 1600 and 2000, the boat was in BF 3194, and at 2030, in BF 3198, the hospital-ship returned, going north.

Facts

Whether there had been a torpedo malfunction or not, I really cannot say, but it is hardly relevant, as this was just another shot into the blue.

Taking into consideration both the stated weather conditions and that the boat was a periscope depth, the entries "...a laden freighter of 5,000 GRT on positive data" and "distance 80 hectometres" cannot be anything but false.

Comment/explanation

The visible horizon form a submerged U-boat, with its periscope extended to three feet above the water-line, will be at a distance of about 3,000 metres, provided that the weather is good and there is clear visibility. It, therefore, follows that he could not possibly have seen "the shadows of steamers appearing through the sheets of rain at a distance of 8,000 metres." It is equally impossible to determine the tonnage of a "shadow" under these circumstances, or its position relative to some other "shadows" which "sometimes appear."

One must also take into consideration the entries made during the following three days.

As per KTB entries 18/19/20-8-44

At 1600, in BF 3188, we are told that two convoys passed at great distance at 1200 and 1430, but there was no opportunity for an attack.

Twenty-four hours later, at 1600 of the nineteenth, in BF 3197, a north steering convoy passed at great distance. Opposing current did not permit an approach. The convoy consisted of freighters and large landing boats. No other traffic had been observed.

On the twentieth, at 1200, in BF 3198, another convoy heading south, passed at great distance in the east.

Comment/explanation

Here we have four convoys within forty-four hours in greatly improved weather conditions and calm seas. In each case the CO stated the convoy to be "at great distance," but he gave no further details. The distance would have certainly been less than the 8,000 metres alleged to have been the distance of the previous target. Why then, did he attack the former, in very bad visibility and with no or insufficient data, while making no effort to do so under more favourable circumstances, as in this case? Alternatively, why does he appear to be in the wrong place?

On the sixteenth, at 2000, for example, he stated: "Observed convoy traffic during the day in squares BF 3197 and 3198." Strangely enough, these are the very squares where the convoys of the nineteenth and the twentieth "passed at great distance." A competent CO would have known where to best position his boat in order to intercept the targets. This one, obviously, did not.

However, there were moments, on occasion, that the boat was in the right place at the right time.

As per KTB entries 20/21-8-44

The boat was in BF 3199, and at 1640 a sound-band was moving from south to north. There were twenty smallish steamers at a distance of 60 hectometres.

At 1708, the CO fired a T5-shot from tube I at the next to last steamer (1,500 tons) of the convoy. The torpedo struck after two minutes eighteen and one-half seconds, and loud sinking noises could be heard, followed by audible impact on the sea-bed. The boat then moved off to the southwest on silent speed.

Five depth charges were dropped astern at 1720, followed by three more nine minutes later, and another five at 1749.

Some destroyers were trying to find the boat by means of asdic, sound search and Kreissaege. The pursuers' Kreissaege could still be heard faintly after U-764 had moved to BF 3532 at 2000. Schnorkelling commenced in the same square at 2323 while steering an easterly course.

Schnorkelling had been stopped at 0135 of the twenty-first to carry out a hydrophone search. Six well-placed depth-charges detonated, and it was assumed that two destroyers must have heard the boat.

This was followed by ten very dull D/Cs at 0150, by four more at 0206, another four eleven minutes later, and finally two more at 0225.

The destroyers took alternating actions: while one stopped and sound-searched the area, the other threw depth-charges, but at 0335, in BF 3611, no more sounds could be detected and schnorkelling was then resumed.

Facts

It was more than obvious that he sunk this vessel; two dull thuds could be heard hitting the bottom after the torpedo had struck. However, though he claimed and was credited with 1,500 GRT being sunk, the claim is false. The vessel was the SS *Coral* of a mere 638 GRT.

Comment/explanation

At this point, there was a convoy of twenty ships clearly within firing range, yet this man resolved to sending only a single "fish" on its way. Once again, his actions are incomprehensible. If this "attack-spirited" CO saw fit to fire at a mere shadow barely visible through the rain at a distance of some 8,000 metres, it would be reasonable to assume that he would take advantage of a much more favourable situation when presented. Once again, he did not. He may have been apprehensive of the boat popping up to the surface like a champagne cork out of a bottle if he fired all bow tubes into the convoy, however, he still refused to take full advantage of his situation.

As per KTB entries 21/22/23-8-44

At 0400, the boat was in BF 3611 where forty-five minutes later, a faint radar search had been detected. Schnorkelling then ceased, while the radar pulses slowly increased in volume, and a sound-band was heard at volume 2, moving from north to south. Schnorkelling commenced again at 2305.

U-764's route, 7-31 August 1944.

There were too many discrpeancies between courses steered and positions reached to illustrate them all. Two outstanding examples will suffice:

9 August

2000 in BF 2585
2315 in BF 2526
2400 in BF 2583

Course = 60°
66 miles in four hours.

30 August

2000 in BF 1699
2230 in BF 2298
2400 in BF 1697

Course = 287°
240 miles in four hours.

51°N
50°N
49°N
48°N
8°W
7°W
6°W
5°W
4°W
3°W
2°W
1°W
0°W
Brest
Cherbourg
5,000 GRT attacked, missed.
Boat attacked by A/S hunters
LCT's attacked. None sunk.
August

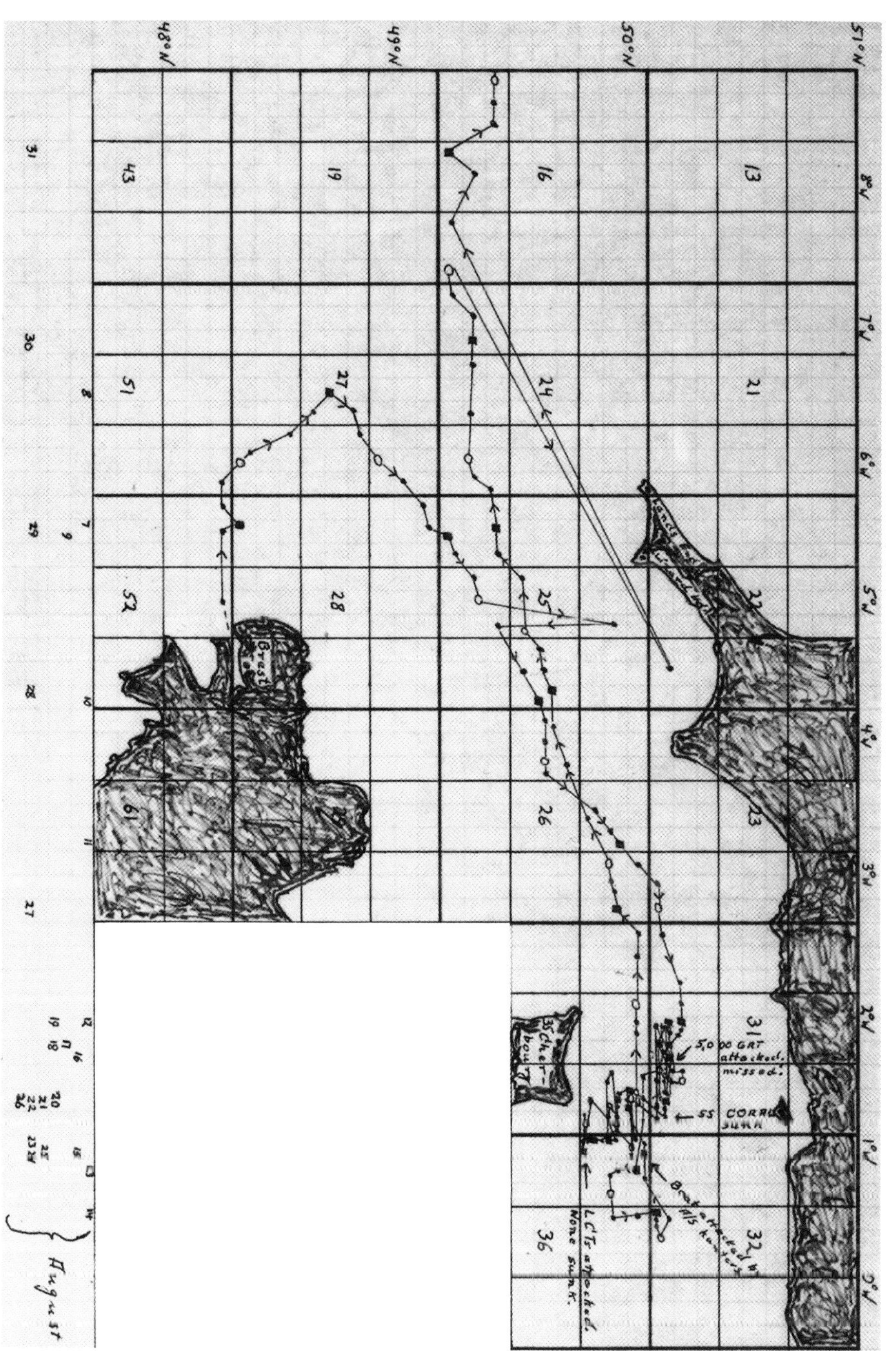

Chart Nine

From 0800 of the twenty-first to 0000 of the twenty-second, the boat remained in BF 3532. No convoy traffic had been observed; instead, there were more patrols about.

Schnorkelling had been interrupted from 0110 to 0210 because two patrol vessels were passing very close to the boat at creeping speed from east to west. Schnorkelling was resumed until 0422.

From 0400 to 1200, the boat was in BF 3535, at 1600 in BF 3536, back to BF 3535 at 2000, and schnorkelling commenced again at 2339 in BF 3536. Apart from constant patrol activities, no traffic had been observed.

At 0324 of the twenty-third, schnorkelling ceased in BF 3614, and at 0600, in the same square, a south-steering convoy was heard by hydrophone, but there was no attack due to darkness.

At 0800, the boat was in BF 3614, at 1200 and 1600 in BF 3534, and at 2000 in BF 3536, where at dusk, at 2030, a north-steering convoy had been noticed at great distance.

All day long there were extensive activities by search groups using asdic, Kreissaege, sound search, rattle and knocker. Many D/Cs had also been dropped. But convoys in this part of the operational area were found to be passing during the hours of dawn and dusk only. The attack area had been moved farther to the south.

Comment/explanation

At 2030, he stated that the attack area had been moved farther to the south, but that does not appear to have been the case. At 0000 of the twenty-fourth, the boat was still in the same square and it was not until 0300, that the position had changed to BF 3617.

On the sixteenth, at 2000, he had stated that convoy traffic had been observed during the day in BF 3197 and BF 3198, but after having missed the freighter of, allegedly, 5,000 GRT in BF 3197 on the seventeenth, he moved out of the area and then floated about for sixteen hours (1600 of the eighteenth to 0800 of the nineteenth) in BF 3188.

By so doing, he completely ignored the orders given by W/T 1750 on 11 June, which stated that the boats in attacking areas were to lie on the bottom for as long as possible, in order to cut down on the time required for recharging batteries; the danger from mines is less than that from the air. At routine times for VLF-transmission, boats are to go to receiving depth. This man, however, did not lie on the bottom, either in areas where traffic had been observed previously (as in BF 3197 and 3198), or anywhere else.

The same applies on the twenty-first when he remained in BF 3532 for sixteen hours, until moving next door on the twenty-second, and then oscillating between BF 3535 and BF 3536 for the following twenty hours.

However, he did *not* obey orders and go to the bottom to preserve battery power at all. And, when he finally did decide to become active, he made another mess of the situation.

As per KTB entries 24/25-8-44

At 0700, in BF 3617, a wide sound-band was heard to the north. Fifteen minutes after, a convoy, consisting of about twenty landing craft of some 3,000 tons each, was approaching from that direction on a course of 160° true.

The sea was like a duckpond, and at 0730, the CO fired two LUTs from tubes I & II, and missed.

We are told that the torpedo in tube II started running while still in the tube, because the data transmission gear had not retracted, and the torpedo had been pushed out by means of the mine ejector. The miss from tube I was unexplained; the data had been positive.

After firing, the upper edge of the conning tower broke the surface at a distance of 300 metres from the nearest vessel, but there was no counter-attack.

On the next day, the twenty-fifth, at 0600 in the same square, a sound-band was again approaching from the north, and forty-five minutes later, the boat found itself within a multitude of landing craft.

At 0704, the CO fired a T5 from tube IV at a landing craft of 350 tons, and had another unexplained miss on positive data.

A minute later, he fired a further T5 from the stern tube at a funnel-type tank landing craft of 350 tons. This shot was followed by a detonation and sinking noises three minutes after firing. Ten minutes thereafter, propeller noises of a motor boat were heard near the spot of sinking. This was assumed to be a rescue boat.

There was again no counter-attack, and U-764 moved off to the west.

Facts

The CO's attack of the twenty-fifth failed to sink the targets just as much as his attempt on the previous day, for his claim of having sunk this landing craft is false.

The vessel concerned was LCT 1074; however, it was not even realized that a torpedo attack had taken place. Instead, the assumption was that it had struck a mine in a channel believed to have been swept. Its stern had been blown off, but the bow section was towed to Utah Station ship *T.B. Robertson* by LCT 800, where the survivors received medical attention.

Comment/explanation

As the damage to the LCT had been mistakenly attributed to the craft having hit a mine, this would explain the absence of a counter-attack, at least at that time. And the CO neither observed the result of his shot, nor the arrival of a rescue-ship, as entries are nothing but guesswork, anyway.

However, one must not overlook the fact that twenty-four hours earlier there was an end-of-run detonation, plus a U-boat's conning tower breaking surface as close as 300 metres to the nearest vessel, and at this point there were two further detonations in the very same area. Although one of those had been taken as having been caused by a mine, the classification that had been given to the end-of-run detonation of the first torpedo is unclear.

It is reasonable to assume that someone had put two and two together, came up with the correct answer of there being a U-boat lurking in that area, and dispatched an A/S-patrol with orders to search for and sink that boat.

That is precisely what happened.

As per KTB entries 25-8-44

The boat was running at slow speed, when, at 1810, in BF 3611, it was suddenly attacked by a destroyer which, it was presumed, had been stopped. Three minutes later, while the boat was at forty metres, a series of D/Cs rained down upon it.

At 1827, the boat, now at forty-five metres, received another series of D/Cs. It became heavier quite quickly and slowly fell away, due to a large amount of water which was entering the rear compartment.

U-764 bottomed at fifty-five metres at 1830. Depth-charging then stopped, but search activities continued.

The main damage suffered by the boat was as follows: The attack periscope was out of action, as was the echo-sounder; the exterior exhaust-gas flap of the JU-compressor was torn, as was fuel bunker 2i. The rear door of tube I had been torn off and the coupling gear of the port main clutch had also been torn off at the pressure hull. The cooling water return pipeline in the engine room was torn and the flange of the cooling water board-valve was leaking profusely. The front bearings of the electric motor on the port side were scratching badly, and the main rudder was making loud noises. There was a leak in the cooling water pipeline of the electric motors, and the radar cable was leaking as well.

Several cells of the battery had been torn, tube II could not be reloaded, and both shafts were pulsating. The spindleshaft of the forward hydroplane was bent and making loud noises. The gyro-compass, hydrophone receiver and revolution counter were out of action temporarily, and there were many troublesome noises throughout the boat.

While damage was being repaired during the night, search activities near the boat diminished.

At 0035 of the twenty-sixth, the boat was lifted off the sea-bed and schnorkelling commenced on course west; the stern was still making much water.

At 0221, the W/T 1437 of the twenty-fifth was received, ordering Foerster, Sachse, Bremen, and Reff to commence return journey to Norway forthwith, and reminding these COs of the orders given in W/T 2117 of the fifteenth.

At 0400 the CO stated to have commenced return journey.

Facts

After the attack on the LCTs, all was quiet, initially. However, by about noon, the engine or propeller noises of two vessels, apparently on A/S-search, had first been heard, and the hydrophone operator informed the CO of that fact. He, lying on his bunk, made no move; he merely replied that any change should be reported to him.

This search continued all day long. The hunters' position, relative to the boat, changed frequently. Sometimes one of them stopped, possibly for a better sound search, but they were certainly tenacious in their quest. The CO, however, in spite of being kept informed, still made no move.

By 1810, their efforts had finally borne fruit as far as pin-pointing our position. The first of the hunters, engines screaming, made her run-in from our starboard beam. Only at that point, when her thrashing propellers could be heard unaided in the boat, did the CO lift himself off his bunk to go to the control room. He ordered the helm hard a-port and an increase of speed, resulting in both hunter and hunted traveling in the same direction. This was when the first series of D/Cs was dropped almost on top of us.

No sooner had this attacker cleared the target when the second one made her run from the opposite direction, dropping her load of D/Cs as well. Fortunately, we were in a head-to-head inclination, showing a small silhouette, and had moved away from the original position toward the attacker; this was quite possibly the factor which minimized the damage inflicted.

The boat was then ordered to the bottom, with every thing switched off; potash filters were to be used and silence was ordered throughout the boat. Although search activities continued for some time, there were no more D/Cs.

Comment/explanation

As the facts again clearly illustrate, the KTB entries are patently false.

By the entry of 1810, the CO made it appear as if the destroyer had been sitting there like a spider in a web, quietly waiting for whatever prey might be coming within her reach. The CO, then, totally unaware of her presence, quite unwittingly ran right into this web and was pounced on, and made a meal of–well, almost. Whereas, in actuality, he had been made aware of the presence of *two* hunters, engaged in an active search for the past 4-5 hours. Once again, he was too incompetent to take any action before getting caught.

Having been caught by a well-placed series of D/Cs, he continued the story of a "surprise attack by one destroyer" by falsely stating the second series of D/Cs to have been dropped fourteen minutes after the first. He is, thereby, creating the impression of this single destroyer having made a wide u-turn, possibly first observing any effects of the initial attack, and only then running in for a second attempt. Whereas, as already stated, the second attack followed very close to the first, for the obvious reason of not wanting to lose the target. No asdic having been employed, the hunters relied solely upon sound search, and if they had been waiting fourteen minutes before launching their second attack in waters very much disturbed by the first, then the contact was in danger of being lost again. For this reason alone, the second attack followed closely upon the first and not a quarter of an hour later. Furthermore, if there had been such an interval between both attacks, we would hardly have been caught by the second load of D/Cs in the same way, if at all, for we would have been almost a mile away in a different direction.

In any event, if the CO had been a competent one, all of this could have been avoided. He could have remained near the spot where the attack upon the LCTs had been made, simply because nobody would have expected him to do so. He could have remained mobile for 2-3 hours to see what, if any, countermeasures the enemy may have employed, and then went to the bottom to have the tubes reloaded and prepared for anything else that may have been headed his way. After all, the convoy of the previous day traveled through the very same area.

He would have also saved a lot of battery power, thereby considerably shortening the recharging time during the next night. Indeed, the boats had been ordered to do just that by the previously mentioned W/T 1750 of 11 June, which stated that boats in the attacking area were to lie on the bottom for as long as possible in order to reduce charging time.

Alternatively, he should have gone down to the bottom and stayed there quietly when the search group had first been reported to him; however, he would not do that either. Since the hunters did not use asdic but relied on sound search only, we would almost certainly not have been found.

Once again, the CO, by his utter incompetence, had put the boat and the crew into jeopardy. And, in order to conceal his failings, he made no entry of having been warned of the presence of two hunters since about noon; he then made it appear as if he had been caught right out of the blue by just one destroyer.

Just as the previous mission, only pure luck (probably the loss of contact and no more D/Cs) enabled us to survive in spite of the damage inflicted upon the boat. Yet, none of this need ever have occurred, if the CO would have been cured of his arrogance and obeyed orders instead.

In this context, one should consider the W/T 1726 of 12 June which ordered:

> When there is an opportunity for attack, do not economize torpedoes, not even if prospects of success are meager owing to the small size of the target or because of the seaway. Fire LUT-fans at bunches.

This is precisely what he should have done!

On the seventeenth, he fired once from the stern tube at a freighter of allegedly, 5,000 GRT—and missed. He could have, in addition, fired the four bow torpedoes at brief intervals into the convoy as well. He did not.

Between 1600 of the eighteenth and 1200 of the twentieth, there were four convoys. He claimed that they were "at great distance" and, therefore, did not shoot. But at 1708, on the same date, he did fire one single "fish" at a convoy, sinking SS *Coral* in the process. It is impossible to determine what his reasoning was for firing only once. The opportunities were there, and he would have been fully justified in expending all torpedoes on, say, three or four of those six convoys (he may have even hit something), thus concluding the mission and then proceeding to Norway as per W/T 2107 of the fifteenth, undamaged.

The mental capacity of this man is further questioned by the fact that he did not even learn from his own experience or take it into consideration. After the previous mission, both he and OL Stuckmann had been ordered to report to the Commander-in-Chief in person, which resulted in the W/T 2025 of 23 June. This related the experiences of Bremen and Stuckmann in the operational area for the benefit of all other boats, stating that there was strong convoy traffic on the indicated routes, which was easy to find because the landing craft were flying barrage balloons. There were great prospects of success in BF 35 & 36 against all manner of targets ranging from battleships to landing boats. A/S hunt was rendered very difficult due to the prevailing hydrophone and location conditions, and it was possible to lie on the bottom undisturbed. The prospect of success against search groups during the approach passage are slight when compared with the favourable prospects in the operational area.

Having ignored both his previous experiences and the orders from HQ, he literally occasioned the attack of the twenty-fifth, resulting in heavy damage. Termination of the mission was thereby enforced in any event, notwithstanding the order given by W/T 1437 of the twenty-fifth to "commence return journey to Norway forthwith." This, of course, had not been received until after 0200 of the following morning because we stayed on the bottom since 1830, instead of being at reception depth for VLF-transmissions.

While on the subject of staying on the bottom, and in the context of the order to stay there as long as possible, one should note the fact that on the twenty-sixth, after the return journey to Norway had been commenced, the CO did actually lay the boat on the bottom between 1135 and 1800. And, he did the same on the following day, between 1315 and 1840. Opposing current was stated as his reasoning for these actions.

At this point, the boat was out of the Channel and on its way to Norway, but that does not mean the end of the false entries. On the thirteenth, at 2230 for example, the position was given as BF 2298. It is impossible to determine what the CO's intentions were, or how he managed to travel some 240 miles in four hours.

As per KTB entries 5-9-44

At 2000, in AL 9637 and under torn clouds, the CO stated his intention of surfacing at dusk in order to transmit the boat's position by short-signal and to take star-sights.

The boat surfaced at 2206 in AL 9682. The transmuter for the 200-watt transmitter was out of action, therefore the position had been sent by using the 40-watt transmitter. The B-bar had been transmitted twice, but there was no acknowledgement of it having been received.

We dived again at 2243, and he stated that the boat had been submerged for thirty-one days.

Facts

It is correct that the 200-watt transmitter was out of action, but there was no transmission on that day.

Comment/explanation

The purpose of using a short-signal is to keep the transmission time to an absolute minimum, thus, hopefully, evading being picked up by the enemy's shore and/or sea-borne D/F. Transmitting the same signal twice defeats that purpose, and the procedural orders (as laid down in the NBU) expressly forbid such repeat transmission by the U-boat.

In addition, the W/T 2339 of 16 June canceled the experiential W/T Message No. 128 and substituted the following:

> It has been found that most enemy vessels are equipped with a short wave D/F-set. They can take bearings of U-boat transmissions on short wave, and such bearings are accurate up to about sixty kilometres, but cannot be relied upon beyond this distance. They obtain a mean fix of the boat's position by co-operating with one another or with the aid of land bearings passed to them (see Standing War Order).

There was no transmission on this date, and the first one did not occur until five days later, on 10 September. Why, then, did he make another false entry?

The obvious answer is that he wanted to conceal, for whatever reason, his disobedience of the order to report his position after passing longitude BE 23 (as given by W/T 2117 on 15 August). He, therefore, claimed having done so twice, but since the signal had, allegedly, not been received, no blame could be attached to him, of course. At the same time, he made it appear as though I was either ignorant of the orders relating to the correct conduct of W/T-traffic or that I was incapable of getting a signal through to the shore station. To the contrary, any ignorance in these matters applies solely to the CO, and at this stage it may be appropriate to refer to some of the relevant orders as laid down in the *Handbook for U-boat Commanders.*

Therein, it is stated, for example, that the

> ...W/T is the only communication link between operational control and the boats at sea, and the Radio Officer (i.e. the 2WO) is responsible by constant supervision for the execution of the orders and directives issued.

And

> ...it is a prerequisite for pertinent and proper performance that both the Commanding Officer, the Radio Officer and the W/T personnel are well-versed in the procedure and knowledge of the orders pertaining to the execution of W/T communications.

This section also draws attention to the danger of a boat's transmission being D/F'd by the enemy, and that even a B-bar is not immune; therefore, any transmission should be kept as short as possible.

Personally, I would not expect either the CO or the 2WO to have the knowledge or the experience as required by these orders. This, after all, is the province of the PO-Telegraphist—in this case, mine!

I had acquired both the knowledge and the experience during eighteen months service at U-boat HQ, but I must confess having committed at terrible breach of the regulations at one time. During my early days at HQ, I did actually call a boat to repeat its B-bar which, due to atmospherics, had been received badly garbled. As a result, the officer of the watch made it quite clear that if, as a consequence of my action, that boat had been D/F'd and attacked or, worse, had even been sunk, then I would have had to face a court-martial. Fortunately, that boat returned to its base safely, but I never forgot that lesson.

I can, therefore, categorically state that I never transmitted a B-bar (or a W/T) twice.

As for the CO's statement of taking star-sights, that may have been possible, but it may have proven somewhat disappointing when one considers the KTB entry "torn clouds." In fact, the taking of D/F-bearings on Irish radio beacons, which were still working as per their original peace-time schedule, had been ordered.

The normal procedure for taking such bearing was to surface, have the lookouts stationed on the bridge and the AA-guns manned. But every surfacing, in particular at this stage of the war and in that area, put the boat at great risk of being attacked, most of all from the air. In order to obtain an accurate position, at least two or three bearings on separate radio beacons had to be taken, and as these transmit at different time schedules, thirty or more minutes may be necessary to obtain the data required.

Having given the matter some thought, I came to the conclusion that there was no need at all for using the usual procedure and putting the boat at unnecessary risk in the process. I therefore, suggested dispensing with surfacing altogether, if the LI could hold the boat for a few minutes, during each beacon's transmission time, in such a way that the upper edge of the conning tower is clear of the sea. By these means, the extended D/F-loop would also be clear and any number of bearings could be taken successively without undue risk. This procedure has, in fact, been successfully adopted and should have been mentioned in the KTB for the benefit of other boats. However, once again, an entry of considerable importance was omitted.

By W/T 0901 on 1 September, we had been ordered to change frequency to the Ireland service as from 0800 on the third, and the first transmission of this mission was made on the tenth by using the 40-watt transmitter.

As per KTB entries 10-9-44

The boat surfaced at 2314 in AL 3494 for transmission of a situation report.

The W/T 2300, transmitted at 2339, reported the boat to be in AL 34. The situation in BF 3617 was said to be as per Rodler's W/T. The CO stated to have sunk a freighter of 1,500 tons and a landing craft of 350 tons, and added that the boat had been heavily damaged by D/Cs.

U-764 disappeared again from the surface at 2345 in AL 3491.

Facts

The success figures given are false. The freighter that had been sunk was SS *Coral* of 638 GRT, less than half of the stated tonnage, and the landing craft, though damaged, survived.

Comment/explanation

The receipt of this W/T, plus that of the two B-bars nine days later (see KTB entry 19-9-44), underline the falsehood of the entry made on 5 September, where he stated that the B-bar had been transmitted twice but had not been received.

As per KTB entries 13-9-44

The boat was schnorkelling in AE 9416, and under the time of 2211, the CO stated that the following serial numbers were missing: No. 151 of the third, No. 149 of the eighth, and Nos. 178, 181-183 of 10 September.

Comment/explanation

Though the entry may well be correct, the question arises as to his reasoning for making it. The obvious answer is that he wanted to, once again, dole out some black marks against the communications department, whereas he also revealed more of his own incompetence without even realizing it. That is to say that I cannot do more than monitor both our allotted short wave service and the repeat transmission on VLF at the same time, in order to catch as many W/Ts from HQ as possible during schnorkelling. If any serial numbers were missing, it is entirely up to the CO to order the LI to take the boat up to reception depth whenever repeat transmissions are scheduled on the VLF-service during the day, so that any outstanding W/Ts may be received then.

This applies all the more, as HQ has repeatedly stressed the importance of ensuring VLF-reception at all times. But, if the CO fails to give the relevant orders, then he cannot blame anyone but himself when six W/Ts over a period of one week were not received, as was the case here. In fact, he stated in his summarized experiences that scheduled transmissions on VLF had been monitored during schnorkelling only, thereby quite clearly revealing his arrogant disobedience of the orders to ensure VLF-reception at all times.

His incompetence is further emphasized by the fact that merely stating the missing numbers in the KTB will do nothing at all toward obtaining them. The correct procedure would have been to add those numbers to our position report in W/T 2300 of the tenth, because this puts the responsibility for a repeat transmission of anything important to this boat onto control at HQ. Without such addition, the responsibility remains entirely his own. And, as per the orders given in the Handbook, both he and the 2WO are supposed to know about the rules and regulations governing W/T-communications. However, when it comes to the application of those rules, then their ignorance shines through at every turn.

In spite of the damage suffered, specifically the reduced power of the batteries and the envisaged possibility of having to scuttle the boat off the Irish coast and the crew to be interned there, we made it to Norway.

As per KTB entries 19-9-44

The boat was in AN 2471 at 0400 and ceased schnorkelling in AN 2475 at 0600. The course at that time was given as 90° true.

In the same square, at 0800, the boat was taken to periscope depth every hour, but dead-reckoning put us still twelve miles off the coast.

The boat touched bottom in AN 2925 at 1137, then surfaced in thick fog and the AA-guns were test-fired. Through a gap in the fog, the lighthouse of Slottenroey could be seen. The drift, after fourteen days, was given as being fifteen miles to the south.

The B-bar, transmitted at 1247 in AN 2925, stated that U-764 was in AN 2485, but that this position was uncertain. Immediate assistance by radio beacon was requested.

The boat was then heading for Marstein.

At 1500, at Marstein in fog, noises of aircraft had been heard close to the boat, which had been preceded by brief radar pulses.

The boat arrived at Marstein at 1540, was taken up by the escort ten minutes later, and arrived in Bergen at 1900.

Facts

Aircraft had already been heard through the fog shortly after surfacing. At 1200, as usual, the 2WO changed the external (plug-board) connections of the cipher machine. I then enciphered the ordered B-bar and transmitted the signal by a top-secret procedure to Norddeich Radio (see Appendix 3).

Some few minutes later, a W/T had been received on the Coastal service, but it could not be deciphered. Reporting this to the 2WO and asking him to recheck the changes made to the plug connections, it was found that he had used the wrong data. The transmitted B-bar had thus been rendered quite useless, since it could not be deciphered by the receiving station either.

In consequence, a further transmission (the B-bar 1247) had been ordered, thus defeating the whole object of my transmission to Norddeich by placing the boat at increased risk of being D/F'd and attacked by the aircraft in the vicinity.

Comment/explanation

This, without doubt, was an occasion appropriate for the use of the procedure via Norddeich because A) the aircraft in the vicinity, as confirmed by the escort later, were Mosquitoes which were quite obviously on anti-submarine patrol; B) such patrol activities would be intensified by both air and sea, as the enemy, after the loss of our Atlantic bases, could concentrate his forces on covering the remaining Norwegian bases and the approaches thereto; C) being mindful of W/T 2339 of 16 June, which drew attention to the fact that "most enemy vessels are equipped with a short wave D/F-set by means of which bearings on U-boat transmissions can be obtained with accuracy of up to sixty kilometres."

In fact, points A and B had been fully borne out by the CO of U-285 (OL Bornhaupt), who arrived a day before us and stated in his KTB on 18-9-44 that he had arrived at 0800 off Hellisoey, but the escort vessel had not appeared yet. He exchanged recognition signals with U-Steinmetz, who was also waiting for the escort.

A third boat surfaced at 0909 in AN 2424. At the same time, he observed nine Mosquitoes attacking that boat. The boat was U-275 (OL Wehrkamp), and the CO stated in his KTB, at 1051, having transmitted W/T 1030, that Bornhaupt, Wehrkamp, and Steinmetz were entering port without escort due to strong enemy air patrols off Hellisoey.

Indeed, the presence of those aircraft had been confirmed by a British signal stating that eight Mosquito aircraft had attacked a U-boat with guns and D/Cs in 61:02N x 04:30E at 0821 on 18 September. It was estimated that the U-boat had suffered severe damage.

Notwithstanding these events, it had been entirely my own decision to use this procedure in order to keep the risk of being D/F'd and attacked to an absolute minimum, without first asking the CO's permission or even mentioning it to either him or the 2WO. In fact, the CO should have been fully aware of the circumstances pertaining to the points made earlier and should have expressly ordered the use of this procedure. He did not, thereby again revealing his incompetence and, probably, even his ignorance of the availability of this procedure. And, as the 2WO had made a mess of the plug connections, thus rendering the B-bar undecipherable, my own small effort of avoiding unnecessary peril to the boat and the crew was totally nullified by subsequent transmission of the B-bar at 1247.

Although the CO had become aware of both the procedure and the errors made by the 2WO when a later W/T confirmed reception of an undecipherable B-bar, these events were simply omitted from the KTB, lest the failure of the 2WO be exposed. This cover-up was easily achieved because nobody would ever know which boat was the originator of this signal.

Conclusion

During this mission, the CO fired six torpedoes and claimed having sunk one freighter of 1,500 tons and one landing craft of 350 tons; in actuality, he only sunk the SS *Coral* of 638 GRT.

His incompetence caused the boat to be depth-charged resulting in heavy damage, as had been the case during the previous mission. By pure luck, we escaped being sunk or having to scuttle the boat while on the way to Norway. And as before, he took recourse in false entries or omissions from the KTB in order to conceal his incompetence and, in this case, that of the 2WO as well.

HQ had been fooled once again, and the comment of the Chief of Operations, Rear-Admiral Godt illustrates the extent of this deception. He stated:

> This was a successful Channel-mission amongst extensive patrol activities, which had been impaired by unexplained torpedo failures. Having suffered heavy damage by depth-charges, which had been well-coped with by the crew, the boat commenced its return journey as ordered.
>
> Valuable experiences were transmitted to other boats by W/T.
>
> Acknowledged success: One freighter of 1,500 GRT sunk, one landing craft of 350 GRT assumed sunk.

Finally, there is one further point to be made. When the CO attacked SS *Coral* on 20 August, he chronicled the event by the following KTB entries:

1640 About twenty smallish steamers at distance of 60 hectometres

1708 T5-shot from tube I

1711 Torpedo detonation after 2 minutes 18.5 seconds

These entries provide information that is truly remarkable because the torpedo used on that occasion could not have possibly been a T5. A "fish" capable of hitting a target at a distance of 6,000 metres within 138.5 seconds would have to be racing at a relative velocity in excess of 80 knots. It is simply not possible.

The harbor at Bergen, autumn of 1944.

Chapter Eight

Escape of the Big One

Sixth Mission
26 December 1944 to 4 February 1945

The damage suffered on 25 August had been extensive and the necessary repairs kept the boat penned up and out of action for fourteen weeks. The main problem was the replacement of the batteries. The only spare available in Bergen had been destroyed to a large extent, by an air attack, and a new one had to be shipped from Germany. The vessel carrying the replacement developed engine trouble, had to be towed into Horten, and its cargo sent to Bergen by rail. During this time, all work had been suspended, the boat had been placed into the floating dock where, miraculously, it escaped the subsequent air attacks on Bergen unscathed.

Finally, after completion of all work, the boat sailed on 26 December for its next mission which was toward the Channel again.

Individual events during the first fortnight may appear to be of no consequence, however, taken together, they will assist in explaining the CO's action on 9 January. Suffice it, therefore, to mention those essentials.

As per KTB entries 3/10-1-45

At 0650, in AM 3516, three propeller noises had been heard approaching form the east, increasing in volume to strength 3, before moving off to the north. Schnorkelling then ceased. Asdic and sound search had been observed from time to time and the boat was taken down to eighty metres. It had not been detected.

Those propeller noises then decreased in 230° true and finally disappeared altogether. It was assumed that the boat was in the passage of the Minch Islands.

At 2326, in AM 2693, the CO stated that the echo-sounder, in spite of having been overhauled while the boat was in the docks, had already been out of action for the last three days.

On 4 January, at 0453, in AM 2699, the KTB shows a W/T without a time, but being dated 3 January and bearing the serial number 813. This W/T was addressed to Bremen, ordering him to take up position in the desired operational area.

The boat was in AM 5251 at 0838 of the sixth, and bearings taken on the radio beacons of Tory Island, Eagle Island, and the Mull of Kintyre showed a drift of 32 miles in 131°.

On 7 January, at 1820, in AM 5732, the boat was on a heading of 180° true. Some three hours later, in AM 5735, a bearing had been obtained on Eagle Island in 116° true, at a distance of 4 miles. Another bearing of 95° true, at a distance of 3.5 miles, was obtained on the same island thirty minutes later, and the course steered was 270° true.

At 2238, the W/T 2137, addressed to Bremen, ordered him to approach the operational area close under the English south coast, as attacking chances were to be found there already.

The boat was on a heading of 210° true.

On 8 January, at 0555, schnorkelling had commenced again in AM 5759, on a course of 270° true, and the bearing on Black Rock was given as 66° true. Forty minutes on, the course was 188° true.

On 9 January, at 2355, we are told that the boat had been taken down toward the bottom in AM 8473, in order to take a sounding. At 135 metres, the exhaust-conduit had been compressed, even though it had been reinforced while we were in the docks.

The boat then moved off on course 285° true, in case surfacing should become necessary.

Schnorkelling started at 0536 of the tenth in AM 8475, and it was found that the exhaust gas pressure amounted to 1.3 kg at 13.5 metres. Smokiness developed immediately when both diesels were running. Schnorkelling was only practicable with one electric motor and in calm seas.

The CO then commenced the return journey and moved off in the direction of square AL in order to recharge on the surface, should the weather deteriorate.

Facts

The statements made as such may be substantially correct, however, the crucial one was contained in his attempt of obtaining a sounding by taking the boat down deep. There was no reason for this action.

Comment/explanation

Whether the echo-sounder was out of action or not is quite irrelevant because there was no reason for taking a sounding at all (none had been taken during the previous mission, when rounding the southwest tip of Ireland while on our way from the Channel to Norway). It was also unnecessary to take the boat down to obtain an indication as to how much water there may be under our keel at that particular location.

In addition, the CO, himself, had stated in the KTB on previous occasions that the depth figures given in the charts were usually not in agreement with the values obtained by the echo-sounder. Therefore, if he was not certain of his position, a single sounding, by taking the boat down toward the sea-bed, would not assist his navigation in the least. Furthermore, there were far better navigational aids available than a sounding could provide.

As already indicated in the previous chapter, the Irish radio beacons were still working as per their normal peace-time schedules; they had been used successfully both then and earlier during this mission (without surfacing), and they could, and should, have been put to use at this juncture just as easily.

There were also the automatic German radio beacons called "Elektra Sonne." "Sun 1" was in southern Norway and "Sun 15" was in northern Spain. Additionally, there was "Sun 20" in northern Norway and "Sun 16" in southern Spain. These were originally intended for the guidance and navigation of fighter planes, since they did not require a D/F-installation; they could have been used by U-boats as well. Indeed, "Sun 1" had been used during this mission, not to mention the fact that even enemy aircraft made use of these beacons for their own navigational purposes.

Ordinary broadcasting stations also yielded very useful bearings, and if all else failed, star-sights could have been taken because the KTB entries show moonlight and stars during the period from 6 to 11 January.

Usually if a man takes recourse to ineffectual means when a more realistic result may be obtained by the use of far better ones readily available, then one should look for the motives behind his actions. The personnel at HQ certainly should have had the basis for questioning.

On the surface, this could have been ascribed to his incompetence, which has already been demonstrated abundantly. However, in this situation there appears to be some sort of underlying motive.

The W/T ___/3/813, addressed to Bremen and ordering him to take up position in the desired operational area provides a clue because the wording of this signal implies that the CO had actually asked to be sent to the Channel again. This presents the question as to whether or not his request was genuine. The boat had already had two missions in the Channel. Apart from a total of eleven torpedoes fired and running, resulting in just two sinkings, on each occasion the boat was heavily damaged by D/Cs or hedgehogs, and we only narrowly escaped being dispatched by the A/S-patrols in return. For these reasons alone, actually volunteering for a third Channel mission does not appear to be realistic in the least.

In addition, he was well aware that there were no more repair facilities nor any refuge left in France, should the boat be damaged again. He must have also known of the heavy losses of the U-boat arm in the Channel due to the extensive patrol activities both by sea and by air which we had experienced ourselves.

Finally, we were into January 1945 by then, the supply lines of the invasion forces had been well established during the past seven months, and no amount of U-boat actions could have made the slightest difference.

If he was not aware of all this, then he must have been the biggest fool under the sun. In other words, he had to have been well aware of the situation and, therefore, had no real intention of going into the Channel once again. It is possible that his request to be sent there was actually just a way to avoid being sent to the North Channel which was, potentially, a far more hazardous area than the Channel itself.

Going toward the Channel and having an approach run that was free of problems gave him a fortnight to think of ways and means of keeping out of that area, though he could not have known in advance what might have happened. However, when going deep with a boat that had been heavily damaged during two previous missions, and, in addition, had its pressure hull cut open to admit the new battery, the odds of something giving way were very much in his favour. He had to do it at that point in time, while there was still sufficient pressure of depth available, for the average depth in the Channel was only about sixty metres; therefore, he could not have achieved his objective there. Besides, he had already been down to 80 metres on 3 January and nothing happened. Thus, he made his attempt in AM 84, before having to turn to port in the direction of the Channel, and it worked beautifully!

By suffering a compressed exhaust-conduit, when going deep for no reason at all, he obtained a legitimate excuse for staying out of the Channel, breaking off the mission, and returning to Bergen. Thereafter, he could state whatever suited his purpose in regard to the consequences of this damage, as verification of it in the docks would be all but impossible.

All that remained to be done was for him to stay out of danger again (which he did, as we shall see), and he would have another mission of at

U-764's route 1-20 January 1945 as per KTB.

Positions at (German time):
0800 = ——— ■ ———
2000 = ——— ○ ———
between = ——— • ———

Ordered positions for SS *Ile De France* and her mean course = — — ⬭ — —

The boat dived to 135 metres on 9-1-45 at 2355, in AM 8473 and damaged its schnorkel.

The Boat was being overrun by SS *Ile De France* on 14-1-45 at 1615 in AL 6924.

Chart Ten

52°N
53°N
54°N
55°N
56°N
57°N
58°N
59°N
AL
AM
Overrun by
ILE DE FRANCE
Dive to 135 m

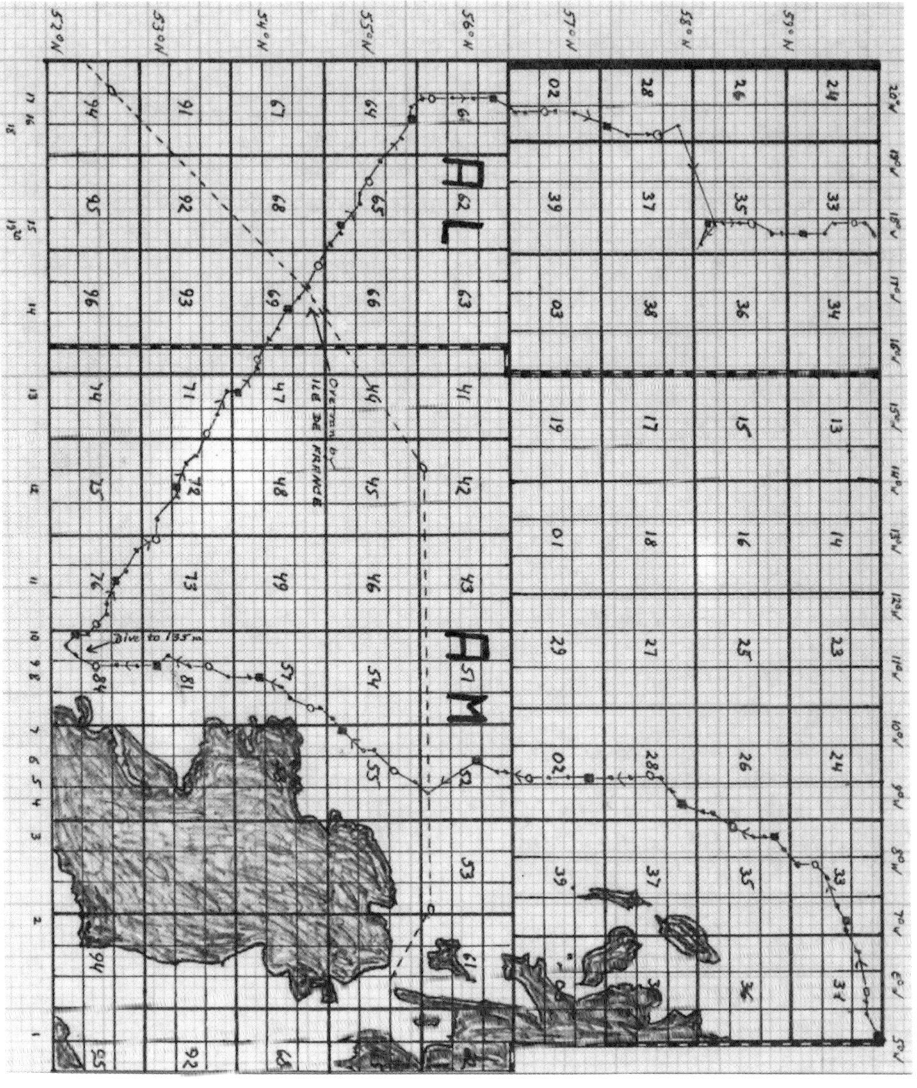

least four weeks under his belt. In fact, by making a wide sweep out to AL 61 (20° west) and then up to AE 67 (64° north), he stretched it to forty days (see Chart 10).

As per KTB entries 14-1-45

At 1615, in AL 6924, the boat was almost being overrun by turbine noises. A view through the periscope revealed a three-funnel steamer, zigzagging extensively, on a course to the North Channel.

The CO stated this to have been a sound search failure because the hydrophone operator had picked up the noise at 1545, with volume 0-1, but only reported it when the propellers could be heard, unaided, within the boat, adding that this had happened shortly before the steamer passed.

At 1700, two further hydrophone bearings on a northeasterly course had been obtained at volume 1-2. Periscope observations, however, revealed nothing.

Facts

This steamer was the former transatlantic liner *Isle De France* of 43,153 GRT on a solo-run from Halifax to the Clyde. She was employed as a troop-ship, and on this occasion carried 951 Army officers and 8805 Army enlisted men. She also had 900 bags of mail for the Army and another 400 bags for the Navy on board.

Her approach had been reported to the CO as soon as discernible by the hydrophone operator, but the former reacted in the very same way as was the case when the search group on 25 August had first been reported to him: he did not move!

Only when the liner's propellers could be heard unaided did he go to the control room and order the boat to periscope depth to observe the situation. By the time he was in a position to make his observation, it was, of course, too late for action. There was no sound search failure, nor any negligence by the operator.

Once again, his gross arrogance, coupled with his general disregard for the crew, prompted him to escape out of his duties and obligations, both as a man and as a CO, by blaming the hydrophone operator for his own lamentable performance. Indeed, in order to conceal his failure and to divert attention away from himself, he repeated this false allegation in his final summary and added one or two others that were equally false. He stated:

> After having been in the docks for three and one-half months, the crew was refreshed and sailed for the sixth mission with verve. Notwithstanding the depth-charges during the previous mission, successes and reports by other boats gave the crew a feeling of superiority. The approach directly under the English coast further proved our superiority when equipped with a schnorkel. Material defects forced the boat to return. The negligence of a hydrophone operator deprived it of a big success.

In this context, we should also take note of a later W/T which, without naming names, has clearly been transmitted in response to this CO's KTB.

The W/T 0458 of 11 February 1945 once more drew attention to the previously transmitted experiential W/T message No. 198. It then stated: "a boat missed the chance of firing at a 20,000 GRT passenger ship, apparently by relying too much on hydrophone bearings instead of keeping at periscope depth."

He did not obey the orders which were given; taking an all-round look every thirty or sixty minutes or so appears to have been too much of a strain for this CO. Furthermore, this leads to another message, transmitted during this very mission but ignored just the same. It was given in the W/T's 1519 and 1718 of 4 January, and stated:

> as a result of bad periscope depth-keeping, even in calm seas, several failures have recently occurred, such as: missing the best opportunities for firing, endangering the boat on account of blindness caused by extended dipping, noticing defences too late, etc., etc. In one case, a boat could not even proceed to a promising operational area on account of the inability of keeping the boat a periscope depth.
>
> The cause of it is the lack of experience and practice of those in charge of depth-keeping under front-line conditions in the Atlantic seaway.
>
> Therefore, all commanding officers must take advantage of every opportunity of training the engineer officer both during the outward and the return passage, as well as in the operational area.
>
> Good advice will not do the trick, only daily practice will produce results.

Comment/explanation

"Being overrun" and "Propeller noises heard unaided in the boat" sound extremely familiar.

Almost a year before, we had been overrun by the port wing of convoy ON-222, and the propellers of those vessels had also been heard unaided within the boat. On that occasion, the CO failed to act. Likewise, one must be reminded of the events of August 1944, the twenty-fifth, to be precise, as the parallel is unmistakable. On that occasion he did not take action until the screaming turbines of the attacking destroyer could be heard unaided by everyone in the boat. The difference was that then, he had known of the presence of the hunters for several hours, and there was no way he could pass off his failure to act onto someone else, as he did in this situation.

As indicated earlier, the CO's main concern (at least as illustrated by his actions) was to keep out of trouble. When the engine noises of this liner had first been reported to him, they were very faint, at volume 0-1, and he obviously hoped that they would remain so and then disappear again. In that event, he need not have moved from his bunk at all, and the presence of this sound source would not have been mentioned in his KTB either. However, things did not work out that way.

The sound source, instead of disappearing, increased in volume, could be heard by everyone, and he could not ignore its presence any longer; he had to do something. His actions consisted of merely going through the motions again, leisurely, of course. By the time he was in a position to focus the periscope onto the target, he was off the hook and out of trouble, for it was far too late to mount an attack at this point.

However, being the kind of man that he was, he would not take responsibility for his own laziness. He shifted the blame onto the hydrophone operator, who would not know of the KTB entries and had no chance of defending himself against the false allegations made.

As mentioned on a previous occasion, it is of no concern of mine whether the CO attacked this target or any other target, or whether he stopped or sunk her, or whether he did nothing at all; my job was communications only. However, when he used a member of my department as his scapegoat, then it did become my concern. Unfortunately, I had been unaware of those entries myself, at that time.

If these allegations had been correct, he could, and should, have had the hydrophone operator court-martialled for "gross dereliction of duty in the face of the enemy, thereby depriving the CO of a big success." He did not do so because not only would the falsity of his allegations have been exposed, but his own incompetence would have come to light simultaneously.

Alternatively, he should have had the man replaced by a more alert operator, but he could not do that either; such a move might have backfired on him in ways over which he had no further direct control. He, therefore, made use of this despicable method of extricating himself from a situation, which, under no circumstances, could be revealed to HQ.

Other falsities chronicled in his final summary include, for example:

> In spite of the depth charges during the previous mission, successes of and reports by other boats gave the crew the feeling of superiority.

Successes of any boats were few and far between at that time, and when we consider the performance of this CO, in particular during the two previous missions, there was nothing at all that could even remotely generate a feeling of *superiority*.

Next he stated

> The approach directly under the English coast further proved our superiority when equipped with a schnorkel.

We had not been directly under the English coast at any time during the mission. In fact, we had been nowhere near it, since he had broken off the approach before even rounding the southwest corner of Ireland (see Chart 10).

This was followed by: "Material defects forced the boat to return."

The material defects (compression of the exhaust-conduit) had been caused by the CO himself, for, as demonstrated above, there was no legitimate reason for taking the boat down deep.

These are merely a few of the relevant false statements in his final summary, but, in the meantime, he continued in the same vein.

As per KTB entries 18/19-1-45

0400 found us in AL 0237. The boat surfaced in the same square at 0545 in order to recharge the batteries and transmit a W/T, but it could not be held any longer by one electric motor at half speed, as the wind was at force 9 and the sea at force 7. At that time, the course was 30° true.

When surfacing, it had been found that the spring of the conning tower hatch had jammed and the hatch had to be opened by force. The assumption was that the spring had been overstretched.

Both 20 mm twin AA-guns, together with their mountings, had been torn off and were lying on the upper bridge. The weapons could be salvaged, but the sea-way did not permit the 37 mm gun to be manned.

At 0530, the wind had increased to force 11-12 and the sea was running at force 8-9, with the barometer being steady at 963 mb.

At 0600, we are told that transmission of a situation report had been attempted on the Diana, the Ireland, and the Coastal service. The time-group had been heard on the Ireland service at volume 2-3; the W/T itself had not been received.

Submerged at 0641 in AL 2898 and continued at sixty metres on a course of 0° true.

At 0135 on 19 January, in AL 2835, the boat could not be held at schnorkelling depth, therefore, we had to surface for charging batteries. The course was 80° true.

At 0149, the W/T 1401 of the previous day had been entered, saying that Captain U-boats West had heard the time-group 0510, at 0634 on the eighteenth, at volume 3-4 on the Ireland service. When the shore station called for transmission of this W/T, nothing further had been received.

Here the CO added: "See transmission on 18 January."

The boat dived again at 0502 in AL 3599, and continued at sixty metres on a course of 0° true.

Facts

The entries of the eighteenth and his comment of the nineteenth with regard to the attempted transmission of a W/T are false yet again.

Comment/explanation

The entries of the eighteenth were made in the following order:

0400 Boat is in AL 0237

0545 In the same square the wind is at force 9 and the sea is running at force 7

0530 Wind at 11-12, sea at 8-9, barometer steady at 963 mb.

0600 Attempted transmission of situation report on both Diana, Ireland and Coastal service. The time-group had been heard on the Ireland service at volume 2-3. The W/T had not been heard.

First of all, his clock must have been running backwards, for the entry of 0530 should obviously precede the one at 0545. Secondly, ordering transmission of anything, while the boat is being tossed about on a raging sea, shows yet again, what a dilettante this man was where matters of communications are concerned. The aerials would have been swamped by tons of breaking seas, and if the station ashore could have received anything at all under such circumstances, it would most certainly have been badly garbled. That kind of information is of no use to anyone, particularly since there was no urgency of any kind to get this situation report to HQ.

The alleged attempts at transmission have been entered at 0600 on the eighteenth. At 0149 on the nineteenth, he entered the W/T from Captain U-boats West, stating that the time-group 0510/18 had been heard on the Ireland service at 0634, at volume 3-4, but after the call for transmission of the W/T, nothing further had been heard.

The CO then links those two items very neatly by adding: see W/T-transmission of 18 January.

In other words, by combining these two entries, he tried again to make me appear to be incapable of getting a message through anywhere, and unable to respond to the shore station's call for transmission, whereas his own stupidity was prevalent, as on other occasions.

If, as alleged, three attempts at transmission had been made on or about 0600, and a time-group had been heard on the Ireland service at volume 2-3, it is not compatible with a time-group received on the same service, at volume 3-4, some thirty minutes later, at 0634.

Actually, I have no recollection of any, let alone three, attempts at transmission having been made on that day. But, assuming this to be correct, linking such attempts with the W/T of Captain U-boats West still does not add up. This entry, therefore, cannot be anything except false.

The CO, nevertheless, continued in the same mode.

As per KTB entries 20-1-45

At 1935, the boat surfaced in AL 3362 for transmission of a W/T. We are then told that twenty-five minutes later the boat was not being received on the Coastal service.

Fifteen minutes thereafter, at 2015, Bremen reported by W/T 1900/20/125 that apart from other signs of old age, the exhaust-conduit had been compressed while at depth of 135 metres. The boat had been on return journey since 9 January. Schnorkelling was possible on one engine and in calm seas only, as the diesels were overworked. Both 20 mm twin AA-guns have been smashed.

Facts

The entry at 2000 is false. There was no transmission on the Coastal service. He failed to report his position in the W/T, in contrast to the orders given in the handbook.

Comment/explanation

On the eighteenth, he tried to degrade my character, and on this occasion, he was making another attempt in the very same direction. Unfortunately, he only succeeded in showing himself up for what he really was.

The boat's allocated service, at this stage, was Diana; therefore, the W/T would be transmitted there in the first place. In the event of the time-group not being received by the shore station, the next attempt would be made on the Ireland service. As the serial number conclusively proves, this W/T had, in fact, been transmitted and received on the said service.

Even if I had tried the Coastal service (or any of the other available services, for that matter) and had not been received, the CO would not know. I would merely report that the W/T had gone out and had been received and only by the serial number would he know what service had been used for this transmission. The statement which reads "Boat is not being heard on the Coastal service" can, therefore, only be pure fabrication.

When commenting on the CO's action of the ninth and pointing out that there was no justification whatever for taking the boat down for a sounding, I stated that bearings taken on ordinary broadcasting stations, as distinct from radio beacons, have also yielded useful results. This is confirmed by the KTB entry made at 2330 on 1 February, which states that the boat was on a course of 122° true, in AF 7965, and that its bow had been turned toward Bergen radio.

There is another point to be taken into consideration in regard to the CO's excuse for his attempt of obtaining a sounding by taking the boat down deep, when he stated that the echo-sounder was out of action. This point had been made clear by the experiential W/T message No. 212, transmitted on 12 January 1945. This W/T stated:

A boat, while approaching the Channel from the west of Ireland, discovered an error of 200 miles in its positional fix. Having reexamined the dead-reckoning, the boat's correct position had been found, and a superficial rule of thumb used by the Warrant Navigator had been revealed. Moreover, the same boat discovered after sailing, that the deep sounding part of its echo-sounder had been dismantled by the dockyard and that only shallow soundings could be taken during this boat's mission.

The moral in this case is that for total U-boat warfare in coastal waters, navigation is a matter of life and death. The CO must draw on all sources and exhaust all aids to improve it and keep his boat's navigation under constant supervision. The absence of "deep-water sounding apparatus is the fault of the boat, not of the dockyard. The officers of each boat alone are responsible for completeness and fighting serviceability of their installations and equipment."

Actually, there are two important points amplified in this moral: A) the

CO must draw on all sources and exhaust all aids to navigation. In this incident, the navigational aides available on 9 January had not even been attempted, let alone exhausted, and, as I had stated then, the purpose for taking the boat deep was anything but navigational; B) The boat's officers alone were responsible for completeness and fighting serviceability of their installations and equipment. This means that the dockyard is not to be blamed for our echo-sounder being out of action. The responsibility does rest entirely with the CO and/or the 2WO.

In other words, if this boat's officers performed their duties competently and carried out their responsibilities conscientiously, the number of problems would have been considerably reduced.

As per KTB entries 4-2-45

The boat surfaced at 0938 in AN 2484, arrived at Marstein at 1029.

At 1041, we find the following statement: "B-bar 1041/My position is Marstein. U-764."

To this he added: "W/T has been enciphered incorrectly."

At 1200, at Marstein, the boat's arrival had been reported to the flotilla via the signal station Leroe, requesting an escort at the same time.

Twenty minutes later, the boat dived again, but was being held at periscope depth while going to and fro at the place of rendezvous with the awaited escort.

The boat surfaced again at 1535, was taken up by the escort, and tied up in Bergen at 1800.

Facts

Not only is the entry at 1041 false, but his approach to Bergen was likewise made by totally disregarding the orders given by the W/Ts 1108 and 1141 on 13 January 1945.

Comment/explanation

Here again, the man was evading the truth, yet by reason of his arrogance, he did not even notice it. That is to say, he was certainly lacking in knowledge, let alone experience, as to the correct communications procedure, thereby proving the falsity of his own entries.

A W/T, transmitted from a U-boat, bears a time-group consisting of time (the time the W/T is handed to the radio room for enciphering) and date; for example, 2134/14. The serial number is added by the shore station when acknowledging receipt by repeating the W/T; for example, 2134/14/129 (numbers 101-200 denote the Ireland service).

A B-bar, on the other hand, bears no time-group at all. The shore station adds time, date, and serial number when repeating it as acknowledgement of receipt. The time in this case being that of receipt.

Even if, as alleged here, the B-bar had been incorrectly enciphered, the receiving station would still add a full time-group (time, date, and serial number) to its repeat because the receiving operator neither knows the contents of any incoming W/T or B-bar, nor can he possibly determine whether it had been enciphered correctly or not. The KTB entry shows neither date nor serial number; it merely gives the same time as the one entered for transmission.

Moreover, if an undecipherable signal had been received, a W/T would have gone out indicating such and stating the time of receipt. Such W/T may possibly even call for a repeat of the signal correctly enciphered. No such W/T had been received.

In this context, compare the W/T 1401 of the eighteenth by Captain U-boats West, which stated that a time-group had been heard, but in spite of a call for transmission, nothing further had been received.

The question to be posed is to the non-existence of a full time-group, as well as why there was no W/T that called for a correctly enciphered repeat. The answer is that the B-bar, allegedly transmitted at 1041, was not transmitted at all.

In order to make it appear as if transmission had occurred, he first quoted its contents and then claimed incorrect enciphering, thereby chalking up another unjustified black mark against myself, while at the same time, diverting attention from his own omissions.

Those omissions were, of course, the ones mentioned in the previous chapter in regard to the events of 19 September, when the B-bar had been transmitted and incorrectly enciphered because the 2WO used the wrong data when changing the plug connections of the cipher machine at 1200. Thus, my own small contribution to the safety of the boat and the crew by, hopefully, avoiding being D/F'd when transmitting via Norddeich, was totally nullified. But there was no KTB entry of the 2WO's failure.

During my eighteen months service at U-boat HQ, I enciphered, deciphered, received and transmitted more W/Ts than this CO had ever set eyes on, and, even at the risk of appearing big-headed myself, I have failed but once, during my early days at HQ. In addition, my service record (which was sent from posting to posting) from both HQ, Petty Officers' School and the Flotilla Communications Office, for example, should have given him more than sufficient indication of my competency as a PO.

In any event, he had the option of rejecting me outright, if he was unsatisfied with those reports or my qualifications. Or, he could have had me replaced later, if my work did not measure up to his expectations. He did neither, in spite of having had ample opportunities for doing so.

PO Schulz, for example, disembarked on medical grounds after the second mission and was replaced by another PO. Having been fitted with a schnorkel, the boat was then operating submerged continuously, and it was found that only one PO-Telegraphist would be required. The CO, therefore, could have disembarked me quite legitimately, and kept on the other PO. Similarly, the boat was due to sail on 26 December 1944, and in fact, did so. But on the twenty-fourth, I was still in the sick-bay and was not released until about noon of the twenty-fifth. The CO, therefore, could quite easily have replaced me by another PO from the flotilla's personnel reserve pool. Furthermore, when I had taken all that I could from this man, I requested a transfer to the Russian front, but he would not accede to my request.

Notwithstanding these points, even if this B-bar had been transmitted and had been correctly enciphered, it would have made no difference, except by underlining the CO's disobedience again.

The W/Ts 1108 and 1141 of 13 January 1945, enciphered in Officers' Cypher, ordered the boats to enter Bergen only during the hours of darkness from then on because of the ever present danger from enemy aircraft. Escort was to be taken up at Marstein or Hellisoey between nightfall and three hours before dawn, and the boats were to transmit advance reports accordingly.

The presence of the escort vessel at the place of rendezvous would be made known by two minutes of short flashes, given with her red masthead light, at intervals of fifteen minutes; the letters "UU" were to be transmitted at irregular intervals by her white masthead light or by a Morse lamp. In order to facilitate approaching the place of rendezvous, the flotilla is to order (without any prior application being made by the boats) the lights at Hellisoey and Holmengraa, or those at Marstein and Slottenroey, and inform the boats by W/T of their operating times. The lights are at peacetime strength.

A pencil note is to be made in paragraph "A" of the Standing War Order No. 425.

Surely these orders are perfectly clear and can leave no doubt as to both their intentions and how they were to be carried out. They were, after all, issued with the safety of the boats in mind. This CO, however, chose to ignore these orders.

Instead of reporting the boat's approach forty-eight or seventy-two hours before arrival (as per the normal procedure), so as to enable the flotilla to order the relevant lights and advise the boat of their operating times, he gave no order for such signal to be transmitted. It appears that he had no need for lights anyway because he had no intention of approaching an already waiting escort during the hours of darkness, as ordered. He went into Marstein in daylight and when no escort was readily available at the place of rendezvous. He then claimed having ordered transmission of a B-bar, reporting his arrival at Marstein, which, it is alleged, had been incorrectly enciphered by the radio room. Of Course! But why is there no request for an escort in this allegedly transmitted signal?

Irrespective of the orders given by said W/Ts, he should have learned from the events of 18 September and the W/T 1030 of that day (which stated that Bornhaupt, Wehrkamp and Steinmetz were entering port without escort as there was a strong enemy air patrol off Hellisoey), or from the discussions of those COs' experiences as to the danger when approaching and entering any Norwegian base. Indeed, this danger had been brought home to him by the presence of enemy aircraft on A/S-patrol the very next day, when we arrived off Marstein during the morning in thick fog.

In other words, he now put his own boat and the crew, as well as the escort and her crew in great jeopardy of being attacked from the air, simply by refusing to comply with the orders given. Instead of making his approach during darkness, he did so in broad daylight and then asked for an escort to be sent out especially for him!

Here the question might also be asked as to why he did not go in, submerged, by himself, instead of hanging about in the Marstein area for five hours, while waiting for an escort. After all, that was precisely what he intended to do after the capitulation–against orders, as usual (see next chapter). Besides, Bornhaupt, Wehrkamp, and Steinmetz did go up the fjord to Bergen on 18 September without waiting for an escort.

Apart from the falsities already mentioned above, there are also some others which, as previously, come under the heading "Incompetent or sloppy log-keeping."

The entry on 18 January, when his clock had run backwards, was already mentioned; a similar example of this is found in the entry of 26 December as well. It stated:

1857 Released escort.
1814 Submerged.

Though the etmal, both daily and for the mission on the whole,add up correctly this time, it would appear that he lost some 640 nautical miles somewhere, for on 27 December we find these entries:

0852 AF 8757
1200 AF 3746
1600 AF 8742

How could he have traveled more than 600 miles in seven hours submerged?

Some readers may now wish to state what the figure for the 1200 position should have been. That is their privilege. But, I would like to remind those readers that neither on this occasion, nor on the many quoted earlier, are we concerned with what any of the entries *should* have been. The objective of this book is to point out what they are, and illustrate that they are *not* in accordance with the facts.

Conclusion

To begin with, the opinion of the Chief of Operations, which stated that

> the damage to the exhaust-conduit made it necessary to hold the boat at shallow depth. The mission, therefore, had to be abandoned and the return journey was justified.
>
> The CO should have ascertained, by periscope observation, whether the targets detected by sound search, during the bright, moon-lit night of 3 January, could have been attacked.
>
> Due to the gross negligence of the hydrophone operator on 14 January, the possibility of an attack had been missed.

This shows yet again, just how HQ had been fooled since they only had the KTB upon which to form an opinion. Whereas, the facts show that the CO, in spite of appearing to have specially requested the Channel-area for this mission had no real intention of going there.

In order to provide himself with a legitimate excuse for abandoning the mission, he went deep at the southwest corner of Ireland on the pretext of taking a sounding, whereas far better navigational aids were readily available. In other words, he only went deep with the hope that something would give, and it did. Compression of the exhaust-conduit supplied the grounds for the abandonment of the mission and for making a wide detour into the Atlantic for the return journey. By these means, he added another forty days at sea to his account, while simultaneously, without effort, he steered clear of any dangerous situations.

On 3 January, for example, he did not even bother to ascertain whether or not an attack was possible, and on 14 January, he acted only when he had no other alternative. After all, he could not have very well remained in the horizontal when the turbines of the *Ile De France* could be heard by everyone in the boat. But, by the time he had reached periscope depth and finally had sight of the target, he had avoided any trouble again, for by that time the liner was beyond his reach.

In this instance, however, he was in need of a scapegoat upon which to blame his own incompetence, and the obvious victim readily at hand was the hydrophone operator. However, he also wanted to guard against any possible exposure by myself. Thus, by the use of further false entries, such as the allegation of three fruitless attempts at W/T-transmission on 18 January, the allegation of the unsuccessful transmission on the Coastal service on 20 January, and the allegation of the incorrectly enciphered B-bar on 4 February, he made me appear to be just as useless as the hydrophone operator allegedly was. This, in turn, cleared him of the risk of exposure from this quarter.

Two U-boat transmitters: 200-watt short wave on the left, 150-watt long wave on the right.

Chapter Nine

Surrender at Sea

Seventh Mission
26 April to 14 May 1945

Whether U-764 was now suffering from old age as had been reported by the CO in a W/T on 20 January may be debatable since there were still a number of U-boats afloat having far longer time of service to their credit than this one. However, the damages received during the last three missions, both by enemy actions and those self-inflicted, had left their mark.

After two unsuccessful attempts due to further schnorkel problems (sailed on 15 March, returned on the eighteenth; sailed on 20 March, returned on the twenty-third), we finally cleared Bergen at 2300 on 26 April 1945. The orders were to go to the Pentland Firth area, but if there were no chances of success available in that region, we were to go into the Irish sea.

There is no KTB in existence for this mission, nevertheless, we do have sufficient evidence to show that the CO continued his deceitful actions right up to the end of the mission and our surrender.

Facts

On the morning of 4 May 1945, the W/T 0935 proclaimed that the U-boat war would continue, and Norway was the HQ of its operational control.

A few hours later, the partial surrender in the west had been signed, which was then followed by Grandadmiral Doenitz's order to all forces at sea to cease hostilities. The order for the U-boat arm was transmitted in the afternoon of the same day by W/T 1614, stating "All boats cease hostilities."

The surrender was to be effective as from 5 May, and all units in western and northern waters and land areas were ordered by a further W/T, repeated every thirty minutes to "cease hostilities as from 0800 German summer time on 5 May. There are to be no destructions, no scuttling of ships, and no demonstrations."

In the designated area, at about noon on the fifth, a detonation was heard, presumed to be one of a torpedo. After a short while, the CO, in a leisurely manner, ordered the boat to periscope depth in order to have a look at the area. Presently he announced: "Destroyer, inclination 180!" Meaning, that she was showing her stern and was going away from us. This was followed soon after with "Destroyer, inclination zero!" This meant that she was heading straight at us.

Asdic was heard, the boat was ordered down and S.B.T. had been discharged. Some D/Cs were dropped, but whether or not any damage had been caused to the boat, I cannot say. There was definitely no damage to or impairment of the radio equipment. The boat once again eluded the hunters, bottoming later and for most of the night.

The next orders in regard to the ending of the U-boat war were given by two W/Ts on 7 May. The first, with the time of 1152, from Captain U-boats West, was in Officers' Cypher to be deciphered by boats at sea only. It contained the Commander-in-Chief's order that all U-boats, including those of the East Asia Group, were to refrain from any hostile actions forthwith and commence their return journey unobserved. Absolute secrecy was to be ensured in order to prevent any knowledge of this step reaching the world at large at the present time. Captain U-boats West added the warning to take extra precautions during the return passage, lest any boat be attacked by the still operating hunting groups.

The second W/T had been transmitted some nine hours later with the time of 2045. This one was again from the operational control of Captain U-boats West and had been addressed to both the 11th and 15th U-flotillas, as well as to U-boat base Stavanger and the Groups at Horten and Stavanger.

The W/T ordered that all U-boats were to be stopped from sailing and no transfers of any kind between the bases were to be permitted. Furthermore, Grandadmiral Doenitz had ordered that none of the U-boats in Norway were to be scuttled or destroyed, since this was the only way that hundreds of thousands of German lives in the east could be saved.

By signal timed 1200B on the eighth, the Admiralty announced that the German High Command had been directed to give surrender orders to the U-boats at sea. This had been complied with on the evening of that day, and after the signing of the instrument of unconditional surrender, the Commander-in-Chief transmitted the relevant orders to all U-boats in plain language.

The W/T 2043 of 8 May was transmitted on all service frequencies, including those of Hubertus and the Northern Seas, and was to be repeated at two-hourly intervals. It stated that the following instructions of the representatives of the Allies were to be carried out by all U-boats immediately:

> As from now on, all boats are to surface and remain there. The boat's number and position, by longitude and latitude is to be transmitted in plain language to the nearest British, North-American, Canadian or Soviet-Russian shore W/T-station on either the international frequency of 600 m (500 Kc/s), or on the short wave frequencies of 16,845; 12,685; or 5,870 Kc/s using the call-sign GZZ110.
>
> Surrender is to be signified by showing a large black or blue flag during daylight and by setting navigation lights at night. All ammunition is to be thrown overboard, the breech-blocks of guns and the firing pistols of the torpedoes are to be removed, all mines to be secured and the AA-guns are to remain in a neutral position.
>
> Communications both by W/T and by signal flags are permitted in plain language only. All instructions, given in the subsequent W/Ts, as to course and speed to allied ports are to be adhered to minutely.
>
> The Allies have prohibited any damage to be done to the boats and/or the scuttling of same. These orders are to be complied with, for any boats continuing submerged travel will still be regarded as hostile and run the risk of being attacked and sunk.

These instructions had been received during schnorkelling, between about 2200 and 2300 of the eighth, but when I laid them before the CO, he crossed out the whole of it with blue pencil and added "ENEMY PROPAGANDA" to it.

Some boats continued transmitting in cipher, therefore one more enciphered message went out on 9 May. W/T 1130 was addressed to all U-boats and stated that

> the instructions, transmitted in plain language on all U-boat services since 2100 on 8 May, are to be obeyed and that no further enciphered messages are to be transmitted.

Although this W/T had made it quite clear to the CO that the plain language instructions were not "enemy propaganda" as he initially assumed, that did not mean that he would obey orders for once. He called Officers and NCOs together, behind closed doors in the PO's room, and excluded the rest of the crew. He then proclaimed that he had no intention of handing over either the boat or the torpedoes. He pointed out that we could not reach Spain due to insufficient fuel, nor could we go to Germany since we had no charts on board illustrating the mine fields in the Kattegat. He then stated that we would first jettison all torpedoes and then return to Bergen. If circumstances permitted, we would go in, submerged, and travel as far up the fjord as was possible. There the boat would be scuttled while the crew went ashore, and then every man was to decide what to do for himself. Alternatively, if the presence of enemy forces prevented our entrance of the fjord, the boat would be scuttled at a suitable place off the coast, the crew would go ashore by means of their dinghies and, again, everyone was to make their own decisions from then onwards.

Thus, the torpedoes in their tubes were fired (one of the LUTs reversed course and its thrashing propellers could be heard passing close by the boat, and it would not have been the first time a U-boat had been sunk by its own acoustic torpedo), and the rest followed after reloading. Then, a course was set for Norway. During this journey we also strayed into a mine field; at least that is what was said at that time, though I cannot vouch for the accuracy of that statement.

The whole situation, however, appeared to have generated some doubts in the minds of the senior members of the NCOs and on 11 May they requested a further discussion. They argued to the effect that they were married, had wives and children at home, that the war was over, and that there was no justifiable reason for continuing submerged and possibly being picked up by one of the hunting groups, being attacked as hostile and perhaps even sunk.

In the end, though the CO and the LI still wanted to go to Bergen, the majority view prevailed and the boat's course was reversed in order to first put some distance between us and Norway. After all, we had to conceal the CO's initial self-serving plan.

On the morning of the thirteenth, we surfaced at last. I then asked permission to transmit our position in accordance with the plain language orders of 8 May, but in spite of receiving the shore station and calling on each of the frequencies given several times, Wick Radio gave no indication of receiving my calls. Finally, I switched off, went up to the bridge and reported to the CO that the shore station had not responded to my efforts. The CO did not respond to my report either. Therefore, as my work with this boat had come to an end, I retired to the after railing of the lower wintergarden and by chance glanced at the net-deflector.

To my utter amazement, I noticed the connection from the transmitter to the net-deflector having been severed and when I looked at the connection to the forward deflector later (housed within the bridge fairing, access to which is obtained by a tiny door), I found this one to have been unscrewed as well. It was no surprise, therefore, that Wick

Radio had not received my calls! When I reported my unsuccessful attempts at transmission to the CO, there were, apart from him, only two other people on the bridge, the 2WO and the Warrant Navigator. As those aerial connections do not part of their own accord, one or all of the people on the bridge must have had a hand at those disconnections.

Before long, an aircraft appeared, giving directions as to where to go, and the remainder of the events pertaining to the surrender of U-764 can be gauged by the exchange of a number of signals as recorded in ADM 199/2317:

> On 13 May, at 1243B, the A/C LCW46 signaled to 18 Group that a U-boat is surrendering in position 61:50N x 00:26W and is traveling at 10 knots on a course of 238° true. The visibility at that stage was a mere fifty yards due to fog on the sea, and the aircraft requested instructions.

The next signal came from the Admiralty, addressed to U-764 and timed at 1310Z. It stated: "Request of German plain language text of paragraph 1(b) of 0202. And we were told to acknowledge and to report our position, course and speed at 1600Z."

(It must be noted here that this signal had not been received since all our radio equipment had been shut down by that time.)

This was followed by the A/C reporting to 18 Group at 1607B that by reason of its fuel shortage it had left the U-boat in position 61:34N x 01:09W, traveling at 6 knots on a course of 235° true.

At 1955B, C-in-C Western Approaches signaled to HMS *Philante* that at 1243B an aircraft had reported the surrender of U-764 in 61:50N x 00:26W, traveling at 10 knots on course 238° true. HMS *Philante* was instructed to ascertain and report the reason for U-764's delay in surrendering. Some ninety minutes later, C-in-C Home Fleet reported to the Admiralty that Wick Radio had had no contact with U-764.

On the following day, U-764's position had been estimated as 59:10N x 04:00W, and at 1755B, HMS *Alacrity* sent a signal to C-in-C Home Fleet, saying that the U-boat was on the surface in position 58:43N x 04:13W, that an aircraft was circling overhead, and she intended taking the boat to Loch Eriboll.

The next signal, at 2044B, was in fact from the S.O. Loch Eriboll, informing C-in-C Western Approaches of the arrival of U-764 and U 244.

On 15 May, S.O. Loch Eriboll informed N.O.I.C. Loch Alsh by signal timed at 0010B that he intended sailing U-516 (with four torpedoes on board), U-764 (having none), and U-244 (still carrying 10 torpedoes) at 0600, escorted by HMS *Deane* and estimated their arrival in Loch Alsh at 1630B. Although the passage did take a little longer, the arrival of those three boats with their escort was then reported to F.O.I.C. Greenock at 2110B.

Most of the crew disembarked on the morning of 16 May in Loch Alsh (to go into captivity for the next three years), leaving only essential personnel on board for the transfer of the boat to Lisahally. In the meantime, at 0125B on the fifteenth, S.O. Loch Eriboll replied to the signal 1955B of 13 May, by means of which C-in-C Western Approaches had asked for a report regarding the late surrender of U-764.

This report stated that U-764, after having been attacked with depth charges some 5 miles west of Pentland Firth at Midday of 5 May, had slowly escaped westward and bottomed throughout 7 May at a distance of 20 miles south-south-west of Cape Wrath. Enciphered messages reporting the end of warfare had been received by W/T, but during the night of 7/8 May, there were no instructions as to what to do.

Further indefinite instructions had been received during the night of 9/10, but it was not until another 48 hours later, during the night of 12/13, that the plain language signals had arrived, giving clear instructions as to the boat's further conduct. In addition, it was stated that a number of signals had not been received because the CO's extreme caution, regarding the exposure of both schnorkel and receiving aerial, prevented their reception.

This report is obviously based upon statements the CO had made on 14 May upon arrival in Loch Eriboll. However, there is a second document which appears to be a summary of further such statements. It bears no date or indication as to locality, but those statements have most likely been made in Loch Alsh on 16 May and they tell the following story:

> U-764's CO was Oberleutnant zur See von Bremen, and the boat was a type VIIc, built at the Kriegsmarine Werft in Wilhelmshaven. It had been commissioned on 6 May 1943 and has had six previous patrols; the first in about December 1943 from Kiel and the fifth from Bergen, but it also operated from Brest.
>
> The boat sailed on 26 April 1945 from Bergen for its seventh and last patrol with orders to attack major war vessels in the vicinity of Pentland Firth.
>
> On 5 May at approximately 1200, the boat's hydrophone picked up escorts slowly approaching from astern and commencing asdic search soon afterwards. One of the escorts appeared to have stopped for some ten minutes before carrying out an ineffective D/C-attack about forty-five minutes after the initial contact had been obtained by hydrophone.
>
> The U-boat remained at a depth of 50-60 metres, proceeding at speeds of 2-3 knots, changing course at intervals and ejecting S.B.T. Two escorts were being plotted continuously and those attacked twice more, resulting in considerable minor damage, putting W/T out of action and damaging the bilge pumps.
>
> Continuing the previous tactics, the boat managed to escape to the east or northeast, bottomed at about 1500 or 1600 and remained there through

the night to carry out repairs. There were no further attacks from then on.

U-764 had been armed with six LUTs and four T5s, but all torpedoes had been jettisoned after receipt of the surrender signal. As both the drum-shaped aerial and the associated W/T-receiver were defective, receiving the surrender signal was beset with considerable difficulties and the CO had no intention of surfacing.

It is plainly evident that these statements and those made in Loch Eriboll do not match, nor do they correspond with the facts.

There are also the false statements made by the former 2WO in *Schaltung Kueste* and quoted in the Preface; the underlined portion of which reads

when the cessation of hostilities was made known by W/T on 8 May 1945. As we still had contact with the enemy, we moved out of the area in the direction of Norway; and on 13 May, when no further enemy actions would be expected, we surrendered.

Comment/explanation

1) Cessation of hostilities had already been made known on 4 May by W/T 1614, ordering all boats to cease hostilities. This had been reinforced on 7 May by W/T 1152 (in Officers' Cypher), transmitting the Grandadmiral's order that all boats, including the East Asia Group were to cease offensive actions forthwith. These orders alone can surely leave no doubts as to the ending of U-boat warfare, though no actual surrender orders had been issued at that stage.

Kandler's statement that "cessation of hostilities was made known by W/T on 8 May" is, therefore, false. It is correct, of course, that the plain language instructions had been transmitted on the eighth, but in his paragraph he omitted the orders given prior to these surrender instructions. In addition, the CO, in his statements in Loch Eriboll, admitted having received enciphered messages reporting the end of warfare, but added that there were no further instructions during the night of 7/8 May.

It follows then that neither Kandler nor the CO had told the true story.

2) According to the CO, enciphered messages had been received during the night of 7/8 May; as per Kandler, cessation of hostilities were received by W/T on 8 May.

This cannot be possible if either "both the drum-shaped aerial and associated W/T-receiver were defective," or if "W/T was out of action" (since the attack on 5 May), as also stated by the CO in Loch Alsh. Thus, it is impossible to ascertain from these statements whether or not the drum-shaped aerial and the receiver were defective. It is also impossible to know for certain if the whole of the W/T-installation was out of action since 5 May.

Yet again, on the day before, in Loch Eriboll, he is reported to have said that a number of signals had not been received on account of his extreme caution regarding the exposure of both the schnorkel and the receiving aerial.

At this point, an explanation is required as to how the boat's batteries had been charged without exposing both schnorkel and aerial for 2-3 hours each night; whether with or without "extreme caution" is totally irrelevant.

3) It is impossible to determine why he proclaimed, on the ninth, that he had no intention of handing over either the boat or the torpedoes, ordered all torpedoes to be jettisoned and then turned toward Norway to scuttle the boat either in Bergen or off-shore. This certainly contrasts his claim that he had not received the plain language version of the surrender orders with clear instructions as to what to do until the night of 12/13 May.

Similarly, it is not known why Kandler stated that we still had contact with the enemy on 8 May, inducing the readers of *Schaltung Kueste* to believe that this was the reason for moving out of the area in the direction of Norway, when he knew perfectly well that the last contact with the enemy had been on 5/6 May. The real reason for going back to Norway was to scuttle the boat there–contrary to the express orders issued by Grandadmiral Doenitz.

In addition, Kandler stated that "...on 13 May, when no further enemy action would be expected, we surfaced..." Yet he knew, from the plain language instructions given and received on 8 May, that as long as the boat remained submerged, it would be regarded as hostile and enemy action could follow, resulting in a possible sinking of the boat, whether he expected it or not!

He also knew that the real reason for surfacing on 13 May was the absence of any other alternative. It, therefore, follows that both he and the CO were blatantly lying; the latter in May 1945 and the former forty years later, in June 1985.

4) There had been no damage to either aerials or receivers (with the exception of the deliberate severance of the aerials after surfacing on the thirteenth) and the plain language instructions, issued by the Commander-in-Chief, and head of state, Grandadmiral Doenitz, had been received and handed to the CO before midnight of 8 May. The CO, however, would not obey orders to surface and surrender the boat. He remained below and wanted to return to Bergen to scuttle the boat there.

The only reasonable explanation for his reckless and irresponsible actions appears to be that he was scared of possibly having to face a military tribunal on a charge of being a war-criminal in his capacity as CO of a U-boat. Alternatively, he at least wanted to avoid captivity, and going to Bergen would have appeared to be an escape from either possibility. He may have even harboured thoughts of escaping from Norway to Germany, which could not have been accomplished from the British Isles.

In order to avoid going to Britain, he did not give a second thought to his crew, though he knew perfectly well, from the instructions received that as long as he remained below, the boat would be regarded as hostile and the crew may yet lose their lives, though the war be at an end. When he was finally left with no alternative but to surface and surrender as ordered, he took recourse to lies in order to cover up his vain and totally selfish attempt at avoiding his responsibilities and carrying out the orders given. His falsifications were so obvious that they could hardly have escaped the notice of the British Naval Authorities. However, they probably did not care one way or another at that stage, as long as all the U-boats were on the surface and accounted for.

As for Kandler's lies forty years later, the explanation would appear to be the one already indicated in the Preface. One of the former NCOs may have questioned some statements made by von Bremen in his so-called book. Kandler, therefore, published the mentioned paragraph in order to provide support for whatever his former CO may have written in this regard and in order to officially silence any other people in doubt. Should this assumption be correct, then he would have been better off not having his story in print because his memory of events appears to be very short.

Apart from that, even statements that may be considered of a minor nature are not in accord with the facts. He stated (and those statements could only have been made by this CO) that the boat had had six previous patrols, the first in about December 1943 from Kiel and the fifth from Bergen, but the boat also operated from Brest. True, six previous patrols is quite correct. However, he did not sail for the first one in December 1943 but on 26 October! The boat then sailed from Brest for the next four patrols, and only the last two (the sixth and seventh) commenced from Bergen.

These then were the people (at least on U-764) to stand at attention to, salute, and say "Aye, aye, Sir," and carry out the orders given by them because they were *superior officers*. Yet, these very same people did disregard any orders issued by HQ whenever it suited them to do so.

The reader may now wonder what happened to all those surrendered U-boats. Well, with the exception of a very small number of the latest types being distributed among the Allies, all others were sunk in the Atlantic at a later date. I, myself, assumed that the boats would simply be taken to sea, have their sea-cocks opened, and finally take their last dive. This, however, was not the case; at least not in regard to the group that included U-764. The boats were intended to be used for target practice, and this group was comprised of six destroyers, one corvette, one submarine, and five U-boats.

The Senior Officer traveled in HMS *Offa*, the firing ship was the former Polish destroyer *Piorun*, and the submarine *Templar* was to carry out C.C.R. Pistol trials. The corvette HMS *Cubitt* and the other former Polish destroyer *Krakowiak* were towing U-2502 and U-764 respectively, to be targets for *Templar's* torpedoes. The remaining three boats (U-516, U-2336, and U-2351) were towed by the destroyers *Quantock, Pytchley*, and *Fowey*.

The first U-boat was towed out of Lisahally at 0745 on 2 January 1946 and the remainder left at intervals of twenty minutes without any incidents. The trials were intended to be carried out the next morning, and at 0645 on 3 January, HM ships *Cubitt, Piorun, Krakowiak* and the submarine *Templar* had been detached accordingly. By 1030, however, the seaway had increased and become too rough for these trials, therefore, *Piorun* dispatched both U-764 and U-2502 by gun-fire in position 56:06N x 09:00W.

Shortly thereafter, U-2336 and U-2351 were likewise sunk by gun-fire, and U-516 foundered in the same position. Operation *Deadlight* for these boats having been completed, the group then returned to harbour.

U-764 after surrender, on the way from Loch Alsh to Lisahally, 17 May 1945. (courtesy of IWM)

Postscript

The operational staff at U-boat HQ had no first-hand knowledge of the events at sea. They were solely dependent upon the KTBs of all boats to provide accurate information, in chronological order, of the experiences gained, observations made, problems encountered, and the remedies applied to redress them.

Only by receipt of such information could HQ conduct the operations as best as possible, investigate the observations made to institute changes in procedure where necessary or advisable, and attempt to solve a variety of technical problems by new research, further development and improved equipment. It also could, and did, pass on valuable guidance in these spheres for the benefit of all other boats.

If, however, a KTB contained entries not consistent with the facts, or did not show facts in regard to specific events at all, then such a KTB is not only useless to HQ, but it can be positively dangerous to other boats and their crews because they did not have the correct information, or none at all, pertaining to situations they may encounter.

It may be said that the points raised would have been of importance during the war years but are hardly relevant today. I disagree. Just as HQ was dependent upon full and correct information then, so are the researchers, authors, and historians of today.

A KTB (or any other document for that matter) is not necessarily what it purports to be. It may be factual, or it may be fictitious, but the uninitiated cannot possibly differentiate between the two. Any book or article produced, which is based upon false KTB-entries, will perpetuate those falsities, and when taking into account any omissions which an outsider would not even dream of, then it is clear that the result will be totally misleading and will produce a quite distorted picture. Such a picture, unless corrected, will be accepted as the truth without hesitation, for all time to come.

In addition, one must consider that a man will not usually resort to falsehood for no reason, or none that is readily discernible; however, if

HQ could be fooled in the past, what hope does the present day researcher or historian have of shedding any light upon such reasons?

This book's basic purpose is to illustrate the falsifications, both direct and by omission, of U-764's KTBs. It was, therefore, inevitable that the incompetence and insubordination of its Commanding Officer would surface as the reasons for these falsifications.

A researcher will take a KTB at its face value because he has no means of ascertaining whether the entries made are correct or not; even less will he suspect what is being concealed by false or omitted entries. True, anyone is likely to make a mistake or error, and an occasional incorrect time or position given may be lightly dismissed as sloppy log-keeping. However, if such mistakes occur repeatedly then they can only be additional evidence of incompetence.

The watchword for the researcher or historian must be: Beware—lest you be fooled, or fool yourself, and consequently fool posterity!

If it is of interest, the following example will illustrate just how easily this may happen.

In the summer of 1986, a Naval Historian in the USA sent me some information about U-764 which stated that Captain S.W. Roskill, in vol. III, part I of *The War at Sea* attributes the loss of HMS *Woodpecker* to U-764. Professor Juergen Rohwer in *Die U-Boot Erfolge Der Achsenmaechte 1939-45* also lists U-764 as the boat responsible. After further studies, the professor now lists U-256 as the U-boat that sunk this frigate on 20 February 1944.

Here, one may question who copied whom. It is possible that both authors obtained their data independently from other sources, such as the KTB of either U-boat HQ or the Naval High Command. Whatever the case may be, one must not overlook the fact that Captain Roskill's account has been published by HM Stationery Office, which makes it official. Official or not, I regret to say that the good Captain is in error just the same.

If the research into this event had been conducted thoroughly and conscientiously, it would have been quite obvious that U-764 could not possibly be credited with sinking HMS *Woodpecker* because the frigate had been torpedoed in position 48:49N x 22:11W (BE 1862), on 19 February, while U-764 was, at that time, some 125-140 miles away, in about 50:26N x 24:15W (BE 1158), traveling on a northerly course. In addition, U-764's KTB shows that not a single torpedo was fired during its two-month mission.

Yes, it was OL Brauel in U-256 who torpedoed HMS *Woodpecker*, and no, there was no real falsehood involved. There had been a mistake, and it happened as follows. When U-256 reported attack and sinking by W/T, I happened to take down this W/T while it was being transmitted by the boat, and I do remember the last three four-letter groups (containing part of his signature) being garbled. The letters "BR" appeared clear on the cipher machine, but the remaining four did not. As it happens, Bremen also begins with "BR" and consists of six letters, and for some indiscernible reason, someone at HQ seems to have assumed (or decided) this signature to be that of Bremen.

In consequence, on our arrival in Brest, we were given a big reception with all the trimmings, which was really quite undeserved. Prior to moving to the reception pier, however, the Flotilla Executive Officer had come out by traffic boat to inquire the reason for not flying the customary red victory pennants (OL Brauel had actually reported having sunk two destroyers), and there the mistake came to light. Although the flotilla now had the correct information, it would appear that this mistake had never been corrected elsewhere; hence, the false statements quoted above.

The information sent to me by a British researcher is even worse. He also stated that HMS *Woodpecker* had been sunk by U-764, and I have also seen the very same statement in *Allied Escort Ships of World War Two* by Peter Elliot (not to mention several others). This evidence proves my point of saying that such errors are being spread in ever widening circles and are then accepted as fact.

This researcher continued with several other statements pertaining to this boat which are not in accordance with the facts either, for example:

Number of patrols: Eight

(there had been seven)

31 January to 20 February 44: Part of *Hai Group*, looking for convoy ONS-29. The convoy evades the search line. Looking for convoy ON-224. Did not find it.

(*Group Hai* had been formed on 17 February to attack ONS-29 and had been dissolved again on the nineteenth. The convoy did evade the search line, but U-764 did not take part in looking for ON-224, since the boat was, at that time, too far north of the convoy's position. Refer to Chapter 4.)

9 June 44: fired four T5s at destroyers while being attacked. No Hits.

(The CO fired three T5s and two FATs into the blue. He did not know what he was firing at, and, we were not attacked. Refer to Chapter 6.)

15 June 44: Torpedoed HMS *Blackwood*, sunk under tow.

(Torpedoed is correct, but she had not been taken in tow. Chapter 6.)

3 to 5 August 44: Brest - Brest. Defect, returned to base.

(We did not sail on the third and return. The boat sailed on the sixth, not to see Brest again. Chapter 7.)

20 August 44: Sinks SS *Coral* in three attacks.

(SS *Coral* was sunk in one attack; only one torpedo was fired. Chapter 7.)

16 to 24 March 45: Bergen - Bergen. Defect, returned to base.

(Defect is correct, but sailed on 15 March, back on the eighteenth;

sailed again on 20 March, returned on the twenty-third. Chapter 9.)

Surrendered at sea in position 61:22N x 00:36E on 12 May 1945.

(Surrendered in position 61:50N x 00:26W on 13 May. Chapter 9.)

Sunk in deep water in operation *Deadlight* soon afterwards.

(The boat was sunk by gun-fire on 3 January 1946. This is some eight months later and is not in accord with the terms "soon afterwards.")

It is a mystery to me where this man could have obtained that kind of information. To visualize that this is correct and then passed on to others with the possibility of appearing in print to be accepted by the uninitiated reader as fact is very problematic to the more informed researcher.

While on the subject of print, and in connection with U-256, the previously mentioned Naval Historian in the USA had compiled a personal history of KK Lehmann-Willenbrock, the CO of the 9th U-Flotilla in Brest and the original skipper of U-96, which was later to become the subject of the TV series "The Boat." The idea was to eventually write a book about Lehmann-Willenbrock's exploits. This project was dropped, however, in accordance with the skipper's wishes. I have received a copy of this compilation in which he states:

> ...on the morning of the fifth, Willenbrock and U-256, filled with passengers, left and traveled mostly on the surface through the Channel and arrived safely at Bergen, Norway on October 17, 1944.

How anyone, let alone a Naval Historian, could have made such a statement, in particular with a view of having it appear in print, is quite beyond my comprehension. He should have realized that even if U-256 could have traveled through the Channel, it would certainly not have taken six weeks to reach Bergen, especially when proceeding "mostly on the surface," as stated. However, surface travel for a U-boat anywhere, let alone in the Channel, was quite out of the question. We have seen that when the non-schnorkel boats attempted to go into the Channel during the initial stages of the invasion, all had either been sunk or turned back with severe damage.

As it happened, U-256 had been de-commissioned due to very heavy damage suffered previously, and at that stage, was in no state to go anywhere. The extent of this damage may perhaps be gauged by the W/T 2305 of 8 June 1944. This W/T had been sent by the 9th U-Flotilla to the Second Naval War Staff, BdU Ops., Admiral U-boats and Captain U-boats West. It stated that

> examination of U-256 revealed that battery 2 must be changed, the pressure hull is badly dented forward, there is one crack, and both port and the starboard plates have to be changed. There are also bent frames, and the keel is cracked and twisted. The mounting of the forward tubes is in

After release from POW camp, the author in Suffolk, summer of 1948. Note the uniform without military buttons or insignia.

Heinz F.K. Guske, 1 February 1992.

doubtful condition and the torpedoes are jammed. Time for repairs is estimated to be at least twelve weeks.

The boat had been patched up and made as sea worthy as possible to provide the means for KK Lehmann-Willenbrock's escape from beleaguered Brest, and they sailed at 0215 on 4 September 1944.

Apart from the totally erroneous statement of the said historian, another author suggested that U-256 passed to the north of Scotland, though he did concede that altogether three different routes had been mentioned.

From this it follows that neither of these two fellows had researched this particular point, for if they had, they would have found that initially U-256 traveled west, on a median course of about 280° true. Having reached a position of 51° N x 24° W, the boat was turned north toward the Denmark Strait, then turned east through the Strait toward Norway, and, though originally scheduled to go to Trondheim, finally arrived in Bergen on 17 October; hence the duration of six weeks.

As we have seen, there is far too much false information being bandied about of which the above quotes are but the tip of the iceberg. Anyone with both the time and the inclination for doing proper research into these matters could probably fill a whole book just by quoting the errors and giving the facts thereto.

Where does it all come from? Is some of it just made up on the assumption that after all those years nobody will ever stumble upon such erroneous and misleading statements?

There are not many of us left, and the numbers are dwindling rapidly. While there is still time, anyone with first-hand knowledge of direct or indirect falsehood should come forward and speak out, so that the chaff may be separated from the wheat.

This does, in no way, diminish the U-boat arm as a whole, nor belittle the deeds of those who have served conscientiously and performed their duties in the manner expected. But, as I have attempted to show, all is not gold that glitters, and fool's gold only serves to distract the attention from the value of the genuine article.

Appendix One

The uninitiated reader will most likely assume that the equipment of the radio department of a small unit like a U-boat is limited to one receiver and one transmitter for short wave communications to and from HQ. He may, possibly, have heard of radar and the hydrophone sound search receiver, but that is as far as his knowledge will usually take him. It is not far enough.

U-764's equipment comprised:

3 transmitters	200-watt short wave 40-watt short wave 150-watt long wave
5 receivers	Short wave
	All wave (from the shortest to the longest)
	Long & Very long wave (up to about 23,000 metres) to obtain, in conjunction with the direction finder loop, bearings on both radio stations and beacons on the surface, and for receiving W/Ts on VLF while submerged, down to about 18 metres
	Long & Medium wave, including the R/T-frequency of the convoys to obtain bearings thereon
	An ordinary radio receiver, which could be used for W/T reception in emergency situations

Hydrophone sound search receiver

Radar

Radar Detection receiver/amplifier

VHF telegraphy/telephony set—for communication between boats on the surface

Underwater telegraphy set—for communication between submerged boats

Echo-sounder—for measuring the water's depth under the boat's keel

Transmuters—for delivery of the appropriate currents/voltages from the batteries

Microphones and loudspeakers throughout the boat, plus their amplifier, for internal communications. The speakers also carried music from the record player to the crew

Two cipher machines and the necessary aerials and microphones for the hydrophone receiver

Appendix Two

The German Grid Square System had been used almost exclusively, mainly for reasons of secrecy. But its notational simplicity lends itself admirably for entries in KTBs and logs and for the coding of positions in W/Ts and B-bars.

This simplicity becomes evident when we compare the Grid System with the usual notations by means of latitude and longitude. For example:

51° 14' N x 26° 43' W = AK 9992

52° 57' N x 14° 35' W = AM 7196

49° 27' N x 21° 50' W = BE 1671

As can be seen at a glance, the usual notation requires fourteen characters (even twenty, if the seconds were given as well), whereas the Grid System achieves the same result by a mere six: two letters and four numbers.

The normal large squares (Grossquadrate), denoted by the two letters, have a side of 486 nautical miles. Each large square is then divided into nine smaller ones, represented by the first number and having a side of 162 nautical miles. Each of them contain a further nine squares, shown by the second number and having a side of 54 miles, or 0.9 degrees of latitude.

Those 81 squares in each large one will be reduced by two further divisions in like manner, so as to shrink the side of each square first to 18 and finally to 6 nautical miles. These divisions are shown by the last two numbers.

All numbered squares are arranged in the same order as are the numbers on a touch telephone, from top left to bottom right. This is illustrated in Chart 1 where we find the 0800 position of convoy ON-222, on 3 February, to be AM 7196, and convoy SC-152 is at 0800 on 10

February in AK 9992.

Not all large squares are normal ones, as the Mercator-Projections of the marine charts require adjustments of the squares in accordance with the curvature of the earth. While there are ten squares of six miles to one degree of longitude at the equator, these will shrink to two per degree in the polar regions, but that does not really concern us here.

There are, of course, tables and formulae for converting one notation to the other, but there is no need to go into those details. Chart one provides both, and the positions relevant to this book can be readily ascertained by whatever method preferred.

Appendix Three

The intelligence gathering agencies on both sides of the combatants endeavored obtaining as much information as possible about their opponents by monitoring each other's signal traffic. Even the volume of such traffic by itself can provide valuable clues to activities in progress, or those that could be expected to be set in motion. Alternatively, such volume may be used for the purpose of deception by making it appear as if there were lots of activities, whereas there were none at all.

In addition, the more material gathered, the greater the likelihood of certain patterns emerging, thereby leading to a penetration of the ciphers used. Since the main frequencies of both sides were known, all traffic was routinely monitored.

The German Naval High Command, as well as U-boat HQ, did not worry about such monitoring unduly, for they were firmly convinced that our machine ciphers could not be penetrated. We now know that they were very wrong!

Nevertheless, it was desirable to find a method by means of which vessels at sea could transmit at least some signals without the enemy even being aware of a transmission having occurred at all. Thus, the procedure known as "Ausserhalb der Schwebungsluecke" (off the main frequency) was born.

Norddeich Radio was the only shore station operating this procedure and as the term implies, transmission by vessels at sea was on frequencies other than the known ones. As a precaution against discovery of the method, the frequencies were constantly changing, and none of the chosen ones were to be used twice in succession, only short-signals (B-bars) were allowed.

The procedure, briefly described, worked thus: Norddeich will transmit six pairs of letters on four main frequencies. These are then rearranged by the receiver as per a predetermined pattern and both the top and the bottom pairs discarded. Each of the remaining four pairs represents the frequency most suitable for the reception at Norddeich (free of atmospheric interference, for example), and those frequencies may range from plus or minus 60 Kc/s to plus or minus 397 Kc/s off the main frequency.

The operator at sea finds these variations by applying each of the four pairs of letters to special tables under the correct day and month, thus obtaining different values (to add or subtract from the main frequency) for every day.

Having decided upon the frequency to use, the operator then tunes both his receiver and his transmitter very accurately to the main frequency of Norddeich and adds or subtracts the appropriate number of kilocycles and transmits his signal between 0-15, 20-35, or 40-55 minutes of the hour.

There is no acknowledgement by way of the usual repeat of the signal. Instead, HQ will transmit a W/T, repeating the contents of the signal therein, adding time and volume of reception and indicating whether the transmitting frequency had been accurate or not.

Even this procedure was not as secret as had been assumed, for we now know that at least some of such transmissions had been picked up by the British shore stations, though it is doubtful whether any bearings on such transmissions had been obtained by sea-borne receivers via their H/F D/F equipment.

Appendix Four

Allied Vessels

HMS	= His/Her Majesty's Ship
HMCS	= His/Her Majesty's Canadian Ship
HMNS	= His/Her Majesty's Norwegian Ship
SS	= Steamship (usually applied to all merchant/passenger vessels)

Acanthus	HMNS
Acavus	MAC
Alacrity	HMS
Alexia	MAC
Biter	HMS
Blackwood	HMS
Braithwaite	HMS
Brandon	HMS
Bryon	HMS
Chaudiere	HMCS
Coral	SS
Cubitt	HMS
Curzon	HMS
Dauphin	HMS
Deane	HMS
Deveron	HMS
Dianthus	HMS
Duckworth	HMS
Dunver	HMCS

Dommett	HMS
Eglantine	HMNS
Empire Mackendrick	MAC
Empire Macrae	MAC
Essington	HMS
Fame	HMS
Fennel	HMCS
Findhorn	HMS
Fowey	HMS
Gatineau	HMCS
Hotspur	HMS
Icarus	HMS
Ile De France	SS
King Cup	HMS
Keats	HMCS
Kootenay	HMCS
Krakowiak	HMS
LCT 800	
LCT 1074	
Lossie	HMS
Magpie	HMS
Nasturtium	HMS
Nene	HMS
Northern Pride	Rescue-ship
Offa	HMS
Ottawa	HMCS
Piorun	HMS
Philante	HMS
Pytchley	HMS
Quantock	HMS
Robertson T.B.	SS

Rose	HMS
Rosthern	HMS
Rother	HMS
Spey	HMS
Starlight 76	
Starling	HMS
St. Cathrines	HMCS
Strule	HMS
Summerside	HMS
Templar	HMS
Trillum	HMS
Vanquisher	HMS
Vervain	HMS
Vesper	HMS
Wanderer	HMS
Waskesieu	HMCS
Watchman	HMS
Wear	HMS
Wildgoose	HMS
Woodpecker	HMS
Woodstock	HMS

Convoy SC-152
Convoy SL-140/MKS-31
Convoy ON-222
Convoy ON-224
Convoy ONS-29
Convoy OS-68/KMS-42

Escort Group C2
Escort Group 2
Escort Group C4

Support Group B1
Support Group B6
Support Group 10
Support Group 18

Allied Aircraft

Beaufighter
LCW 46
Mosquito
Skua
Wellington HF 153

German Vessels and U-Boats

Adria
Gneisenau
Hipper
Scharnhorst
U-91
U-212
U-231
U-244
U-256
U-264
U-269
U-271
U-275
U-281
U-283
U-285
U-288
U-386
U-424
U-437
U-441
U-516
U-545
U-571
U-598
U-621
U-650
U-666
U-734
U-764
U-963
U-984
U-985

U-989
U-2336
U-2351
U-2502

9th Flotilla
11th Flotilla

Group Dragoner
Group Hai
Group Igel

German Aircraft

Air Group Atlantic
BV-222
JU-88
JU-270
JU-290

U-Boat Commanders

Albrecht, F.	OL	U-386
Barleben, C.	OL	U-271
Bertelsmann,H.	KL	U-603
Blauert, H.	OL	U-734
Boddenberg, K.	OL	U-963
Bornhaupt, K.	OL	U-285
Brauel, W.	OL	U-256
Bremen, H-K.	OL	U-764
Davidson, H.	OL	U-281
Dieterichs, H.	KL	U-406
Foerster, H.	OL	U-480
Hartmann, K.	KL	U-441
Hornbostel, K.	KL	U-806
Hungerhausen, H.	OL	U- 91
Ites, R.	OL	U-709
Just, P.	KL	U-546
Kessler, H.	KL	U-985
Krankenhagen, D.	KL	U-549
Lamby, H.	KL	U-437
Looks, H.	KL	U-264

Lueders, G.	OL	U-424
Luessow, G.	OL	U-571
Mannesmann, G.	KL	U-545
Meyer, G.	OL	U-486
Ney, G.	OL	U-283
Reff, R.	OL	U-736
Reisener, W.	OL	U-608
Rodler, H.	KL	U-989
Sachse, D.	OL	U-413
Steinmetz, K.	OL	U-993
Stuckmann, H.	OL	U-621
Vogler, H.	KL	U-212
Wehrkamp, H.	OL	U-275
Wenzel, W.	KL	U-231
Wilberg	OL	U-666
Witzendorf	OL	U-650

Doenitz, K. C-in-C Navy and BdU	GA
Godt, E. Chief of Ops.	KA
Lehmann- Willenbrock, H. CO of 9th & 11th U-Flotillas	KK

Captain U-boats West

U-boat HQ

Glossary

AA-Gun	Anti-aircraft gun.
A/C	Aircraft
Aphrodite	Radar-foxer. Strips of foil on a cord, suspended from a small hydrogen-filled balloon, reflecting radar beams
A/S	Anti-submarine
Asdic	Equipment for location of submerged U-boats by surface vessels, using under water sound impulses. The term is derived from the initial letters of Allied Submarine Detection Investigation Committee.
ASV	Air to surface vessel
Ausserhalb der Schwebungsluecke	Off the normal frequency
B-bar	The British way of describing the prefix to U-boat short signals: BETA. The Morse notation for it is "-...-" but the Royal Navy has no notation for it, therefore, they call it "B" (which is "-...") plus a dash/bar; hence, B-bar.
B-Dienst	German Radio Intelligence Service
BdU	C-in-C U-boats

Borkum	Radar Detector, wide-band installation
BV-222	Blohm & Voss long-range reconnaissance aircraft
CAT	Counter to acoustic torpedoes. Noise producing buoy towed behind patrol and escort vessels to divert acoustic torpedoes away from their engine or propeller noises.
Cable	608 feet = 0.1 nautical mile = 185.3 metres
C-in-C	Commander in Chief
Cipher	Scrambling of plain text by machine or by hand
cm	centimetre = 0.3937 inch
CO	Commanding Officer
Coastal service	All U-boats in and out of their bases, up to about 10° - 15° west, receive and transmit on this frequency, unless ordered otherwise
Code	Four-letter groups (taken from the code book) representing words or whole sentences of tactical nature, and then enciphered by machine. Examples: RKQJ = North-Channel ULJA = Request radio beacon for entering Brest
D/C	Depth-charge
Deadlight	Code word for the operation of sinking all surrendered U-boats in the Atlantic, 1945-46
D/F	Direction finder
Diana service	One of three frequencies (the others are "Hubertus" and "Wotan") used during convoy operations, but only by boats ordered to do so
Eel/fish	Colloquial for torpedo

E.G. Escort Group

Etmal Distance traveled from noon to noon

FAT Feder Apparat Torpedo (spring loaded torpedo). Also known as Flaechen absuchender torpedo, meaning: traveling in a pre-programmed loop, without being aimed at a specific target; rather, searching for one.

FK Fregattenkapitaen = Junior Captain

Fliege Fly. Aerial for radar detection at 9 cm wavelength

FW-200 Focke-Wolf long-range reconnaissance aircraft

GAMMA-search Searching for a U-boat whose intention or route can be estimated

Hedgehog Projectiles fired in salvo forward of surface vessel attacking submerged U-boat. Projectile detonates on impact, as distinct from a depth-charge which is detonated by water pressure.

H/F D/F High Frequency Direction Finder, by means of which a bearing on the ground wave of a U-boat's short wave transmission may be obtained. Also known as Huff-Duff.

Ireland service One of several frequencies used when a U-boat is in the Atlantic

JU-88, JU-290 Junkers long-range reconnaissance aircraft

KA Konteradmiral = Rear-admiral

KK Korvettenkapitaen = Commander

KL Kapitaenleutnant = Lieutenant Commander

Kreissaege Circular saw. See CAT

KTB Kriegstagebuch = War Diary

1st col. = Time of entry
2nd col. = Position, wind, sea, pressure, conditions
3rd col. = Events etc. plus relevant W/T-traffic

KzS Kapitaen zur See = Captain

L Leutnant = Sublieutenant

LCT Tank landing craft

LI Leitender Ingenieur = Senior Engineer Officer

LUT Lagen unabhaengiger Torpedo. Can be fired from any inclination. Improved FAT.

m Metre = 3.28 feet

mm Millimetre = 0.039 inch

MAC Merchant Aircraft Carrier. A merchant ship, carrying cargo, but fitted with a flightdeck for aircraft flying anti-submarine patrols while in convoy.

Naxos Radar search equipment; centimetre radar detector

NCO Non-Commissioned Officer

NBU Communication orders for U-boats

OL Oberleutnant = Lieutenant

PO Petty Officer

Radar Abbreviation of Radio Detecting and Ranging

Round Dipol Aerial for both radar detection and W/T-reception

R/T	Radio Telephony
SBT	Submarine Bubble Target (Asdic foxer). Container with positive buoyancy filled with calcium hydride. Diametre of 10 cm, was expelled from tube similar to torpedo tube. Floated in water at depth of about 30 m, producing hydrogen bubbles to present a false target to asdic.
Schnorkel	An erectable mast containing both air intake and exhaust conduits, thus enabling the boat to run on diesel engines while submerged
Schnorkelling	Traveling submerged, using its diesels by means of the schnorkel, recharging its batteries
sm	Seemeile = Nautical Mile
S.O.E.	Senior Officer of the Escort
T5	Also known as Zaukoening = Wren. In the Royal Navy known as GNAT = German Navy Acoustic Torpedo.
Thetis	Radar foxer, lowered into and floating upon the sea
VLF	Very Low Frequency. Used for W/T-reception while submerged down to about 18 metres
Wintergarden	Platform for AA-guns
1WO / 2WO	First / Second Watch Officer
W/T	Wireless Telegraphy or Wireless Telegram/Signal
Zaunkoenig	Wren – T5 torpedo
ZZ	Distance from ...

Reference List

Ministry of Defence, Naval Branch, London

Code-Book for Short-Signals.

Communications Orders for U-Boats (NBU).

KTBs of U-Boat Command.

KTBs of U-764, 26 October 1943 to 4 February 1945. (Also obtained from the National Archives in Washington, DC for dates 17 January 1944 through 4 February 1945.)

KTBs of U-91, U-212, U-256, U-269, U-275, U-281, U-386, U-437, U-441, U-650, U-953, U-963, U-984, U-985, U-989.

Sailing instructions and positions for SS *Ile De France*, dated 11 January 1945.

Public Records Office, Kew, London. Files of the British Admiralty

Anti-Submarine Reports for the years 1943, 1944, 1945; ADM 199.

British Aircraft Reports, Channel/Biscay area, May-June 1944; ADM 223.

Convoy Reports of SL-140/MKS-31, ON-222, SC-152, ONS-29, and ON-224; ADM 199, 217, and 223.

Decripted Intelligence dated 1 March 1944 to 8 May 1945; ADM 223.

Report of the loss of HMS *Blackwood* and subsequent attack on suspected U-Boat, dated 15 June 1944, by the Commanding Officer of HMS *Duckworth*; ADM 199.

Sinking of U-764 during Operation *Deadlight* on 2 January 1946; ADM 1 and 116.

Wireless Communications to and from U-Boat Command dated 26 October 1943 to 9 May 1945; DEFE 3.

War Diaries of British Home Commands

Report of Damage to LCT-1074 on 25 August 1944 (initially presumed to have struck a mine, but had her stern blown off by a torpedo from U-764).

Reports of the Surrender of U-764 dated 13, 14, and 15 May 1945; plus brief condensation of statements made by von Bremen.

Photographs

Maritime Command Museum/Department of Defence, Halifax, Canada.

Trustees of the Imperial War Museum, London; Crown Copyright, Imperial War Museum.

Index